365
ways to Live
Happy

365 ways to Live Happy

Simple Ways to Find Joy Every Day

Meera Lester

A **adams**media

Avon, Massachusetts

Published by
Adams Media, a division of F+W Media, Inc.
57 Littlefield Street, Avon, MA 02322. U.S.A.
www.adamsmedia.com

ISBN 10: 1-60550-028-3
ISBN 13: 978-1-60550-028-7

Printed in the United States of America.

10 9 8 7 6 5 4 3 2 1

Library of Congress Cataloging-in-Publication Data
is available from the publisher.

This publication is designed to provide accurate and authoritative information with regard to the subject matter covered. It is sold with the understanding that the publisher is not engaged in rendering legal, accounting, or other professional advice. If legal advice or other expert assistance is required, the services of a competent professional person should be sought.

     —From a *Declaration of Principles* jointly adopted by a Committee of the American Bar Association and a Committee of Publishers and Associations

Many of the designations used by manufacturers and sellers to distinguish their product are claimed as trademarks. Where those designations appear in this book and Adams Media was aware of a trademark claim, the designations have been printed with initial capital letters.

This book is available at quantity discounts for bulk purchases.
For information, please call 1-800-289-0963.

TO MY READERS:

If happiness is the meaning and
purpose of life as the great philosopher
Aristotle supposed, then we must be
happy for all that comes into our life,
for even misfortune blesses us if it
builds our character and strengthens
our faith in pursuing that which is
good and noble.

CONTENTS

ACKNOWLEDGMENTS

For Paula Munier, whose mind is a restless voyager drawing inspiration from every nook and cranny of life, and who stands as an inspiration and an exemplar of happiness to all of us who know her.

For Andrea Norville, whose excellent organizational and editing skills vastly improved the manuscript.

And finally, for everyone at Adams Media, who made the publication of this book possible.

Introduction

What is it that makes you happy and contented? Although happiness and life satisfaction are relatively new areas of psychology study, research suggests that it's not external objects like cars, luxury homes, and all the must-have gadgets money can buy that make people happy, but rather internal factors like good health and an optimistic, hopeful outlook. Johann Wolfgang von Goethe, the eighteenth-century playwright, had nine requisites for a happy, contented life. First was health, in order to make work a pleasure. Then came wealth to support one's needs. Other factors in his list included strength to deal with difficulty, grace to confess and abandon sin, patience, charity, love, faith, and hope.

What does it take for you to feel that things are going well and that you are flourishing? These are ideas worth examining, for the answers reveal how you can have a happier life. If you are curious about your own level of happiness, take the following quiz.

QUIZ: **How Happy Are You?**

Answer the questions in this fun, short quiz to discover your level of happiness and contentment with your life. Just pick the answer that best aligns with your beliefs and lifestyle choices and find out if you are an optimist, a realist, or a pessimist.

1. How satisfied are you with your personal relationships (that is, with family, friends, and spouse or significant other)?
   A. I am very satisfied with my personal relationships.
   B. I am neither satisfied nor dissatisfied but feel fortunate to have them.
   C. I am dissatisfied.

2. If you could change your life in any way you wanted, how much of it would you change?
   A. Very little; I am happy with my life and the choices I've made.
   B. I would change several things if I saw that certain areas would work better once I'd made improvements.
   C. I would change a lot; nothing in my life seems to be working.

3. Thinking about the level of stress in your life, how would you rate the level of stress you feel?
   A. Low; not much stresses me out.
   B. Medium; the stressors in my life are not constant but ebb and flow.
   C. High; most of the time it seems that my life is driven by high drama and unrelenting stress.

4. Comparing your life to that of most other people, how would you describe yours?
   A. I am extremely fortunate.
   B. I am somewhat fortunate.
   C. My life is the pits.

5. How much would you change your physical appearance if you had no monetary or other restriction?
   A. Nothing; I am content with the way I look.
   B. A little nip here and a tuck there could make a vast improvement.
   C. I'd change my whole appearance, get the works.

6. How happy or satisfied are you in your choice of job or career?
   A. I am extremely satisfied with my choice for my life's work.
   B. I am somewhat satisfied, but I might be tempted to switch jobs in the future.
   C. I hate my job, and it's a drag having to show up for work every day.

7. When you think about all the various aspects of your life, how would you rate your satisfaction with your life in general?
   A. I am highly satisfied with my life.
   B. I am moderately satisfied with my life but planning to make a few small changes to improve it.
   C. I am totally dissatisfied with my life; it sucks.

8. Rate how difficult or easy it is for you to achieve personal goals.
   A. I frequently set goals, stay focused, and finish what I start; my goals are usually easy to reach.
   B. I sometimes set goals and although many are challenging, I strive to attain them.
   C. I resist setting goals since I never seem to attain them.

9. Comparing your life to that of most other people, in general, how do you feel about yours?
   A. I feel extremely fortunate.
   B. I feel somewhat fortunate.
   C. I feel dissatisfied with my life and can't understand why nothing ever seems to go my way.

10. Imagine your ideal life. How close do you feel you are to having your ideal?
   A. I am living life to the fullest and enjoying every minute of it, so I'd say that I'm close to having the perfect life.
   B. I'm still tweaking with areas of my life. Since there's always room for improvement, I'd say I am somewhat close to having my ideal life.
   C. My life at present is not close at all to what I'd like my ideal life to be.

SCORING:

So are you an optimist, a realist, or a pessimist?
For every **A** answer, give yourself 3 points.
For every **B** answer, give yourself 2 points.
For every **C** answer, give yourself 1 point.

21 to 30 points: You are have an optimistic outlook and are generally satisfied with your life.
11 to 20 points: You are realist and understand that the good things in your life balance out the bad. You believe the course of your life can change and that you hold the power to make it change.
1 to 10 points: You tend toward pessimism and might be concerned that your life is not under your control but is driven by forces more powerful than you.

Based on your responses to the questions, you may discover that you already are an optimist and, if so, good for you. Use the ideas in this book to increase your happiness and spread the joy. If you are realist, think about incorporating many of the suggestions in this book to make your life more enjoyable. Finally, if you tend toward pessimism, understand that shifting away from negative thinking requires a consciousness of how you tend to immediately react to people, circumstances, and events in your life as well as a desire to see life more cheerfully, positively, and optimistically. Mine this book for ideas that appeal to you. Focus on making yourself happy first. Then, express goodwill to others.

CHAPTER 1

Be Happy
with Yourself

Choose to Think Happy Thoughts

If you want to find happiness and add years to your life, think happy thoughts. When you choose positive thoughts over negative ones, you are more likely to develop an optimistic outlook on life. According to happiness researchers such as Martin E. P. Seligman, director of the Positive Psychology Center at the University of Pennsylvania, and Barbara Fredrickson, PhD, professor of psychology at the University of North Carolina at Chapel Hill, positive people generally have higher levels of optimism and life satisfaction and live longer. In a BBC News report, Dr Seligman was quoted as saying that he believed that "we have compelling evidence that optimists and pessimists will differ markedly in how long they live." Dr. Fredrickson has counseled that changing your mindset can change your body chemistry. She has stated that positive feelings literally can open the heart and mind. And there's more good news. Even if you aren't normally a happy person, thinking happy thoughts is a skill that can be learned. Work on being open, being an optimist, choosing to think positive thoughts, and seeing the proverbial glass half full rather than half empty. The next time you are in line at the post office and someone cuts in front of you or says something rude, resist the urge to respond with anger, which can clamp down your blood vessels and increase your blood pressure. Instead, return rudeness with kindness and respect. Keep that positive vibe going through your intentions and actions in whatever you do. The more frequently you choose to be happy, the more your effort will be strengthened. So don't fret; be happy and live longer.   ☺

2 Smile More Often

Force yourself to smile. Try it; it's not that difficult. Now hold it for a count of ten and deepen it. Mentally affirm, "I am happy, totally, blissfully happy." Notice how your mood begins to shift. You can't help but feel a little lighter. Use your smile to start a happiness epidemic. Smile at everyone, everywhere. People are hardwired to respond to the facial expressions they encounter. If you glower at someone, that person will return a frown, but your smile will evoke a smile. You'll feel happier, too, because your body responds to your smile, even if you are faking the grin. So fake it until you genuinely feel happy. Once you know it works, do it often.   ☺

3 Set out a Bowl of Freshly Crushed Lavender

Whenever you have a bad day, feel exasperated, and struggle to get out of a foul mood, use some lavender to restore your serenity. Lavender is one of aromatherapy's most popular scents. Scents like lavender, citrus, rose, and sandalwood can trigger particular memories or experiences associated with them. That's because your olfactory nerve carries the scent straight to your brain. Use freshly crushed flowers set out in bowl, insert some reeds in a diffuser pot with lavender essential oil, light some lavender-scented candles, or put out some sachets of dried lavender. Allow the scent to lift your mood and remember that you never have to live a bad day over again.   ☺

Be Happy with Yourself

Change One of Your Faults

Everyone has faults, but that doesn't mean you are stuck with yours. Pick one you would like to change or eliminate. Take time to do a little self-examination with complete honesty. Do you frequently gossip? Do you have a quick temper and a short fuse? Do you procrastinate and avoid facing problems until they snowball out of control? Or, are you still blaming others for the things that are wrong with your life? Choose to fix what you don't like about yourself. See goodness in yourself and others. Allow your inner strength and joy to be at the heart of who you are. ☺

 ### Don't Harbor a Grudge

Holding on to anger, resentment, and hostility hurts you, psychologically, emotionally, and physically. Even if the inciting incident happened only yesterday, the person you are mad at may not even remember the incident, so what's the point? Don't give over your power to have positivity in your life just to harbor a grudge. Find a way to move past it. Take an anger management class or read books offering specific strategies for dealing with anger issues. Take extremely good care of yourself, loving and respecting yourself enough to ensure that you don't flounder but rather flourish. ☺

6 Cultivate Hope When Disaster Hits

If something isn't going well in your life—your child becomes ill, a car broadsides yours in the parking lot, you overdraw your bank account, or the taxi you are riding in on the way to the most important meeting of your life gets ensnarled in traffic—have hope that circumstances will shift and the situation will improve or be resolved. Find the courage to work to change what isn't good right now. Rather than allowing stress and anxiety to fill you with worry and stress, try to feel hopeful. It will be better for you emotionally and physically. ☺

 7   Praise Yourself

You praise your children, your friends, your coworkers, and your spouse whenever they accomplish something praiseworthy, so why not give yourself a one-minute praising for your own achievements? You're not being a braggart or egotistical when you acknowledge some wonderful task or breakthrough you made during your day. You undoubtedly work very hard and probably accomplish much that no one but you recognizes. If you finally played a complicated piano libretto all the way through or found an ingenious way to increase the family budget, tell yourself how wonderfully brilliant and accomplished

you are. Bask in the glory of that moment. You deserve it. ☺

8   Put a Picture of Yourself (as Younger, Thinner, Happier) on Your Desk

Gaze at an image of yourself looking fabulous. It can move a mountain of negative thought, boost your self-esteem, and make you feel good. Find a picture of yourself when you felt most happy and alive. Frame it and put it where you can easily see it. You have pictures, but none that are that great? No problem. Use graphics painting programs or digital image tools to rework your scanned photo or digital image. Erase some of those wrinkles, add some hair, shift the curves, and turn back the clock. Have fun creating a fabulous-looking new you. Gaze at the photo when you need a little dose of happiness. Let it spark some good vibes. ☺

9 Quiet Your Mind Before Starting Your Day

Focus on your thinking at the start of every day. Are your thoughts already racing through your to-do list? Are they jumping from one subject to another through thought associations? Did a troubling dream leave you anxious or angry or fearful upon awakening? If you answered yes to any of those questions, spend ten minutes before you even get out of bed doing a mental check-in. Take deep breaths and be aware of your entire body. Feel anchored and centered in it. Quiet your mind. Think positive thoughts. Dial out the emotions of bad dreams and the anxieties associated with the day ahead. Relax into peace. The world can wait for ten minutes. ☺

10 Write Three Things You Love about Yourself

Do you have an inner critic that constantly reminds you that your nose is too big or your hips are too wide or your chest is too flat? Think of three wonderful things that you love about yourself and write them on a card. They don't have to be your physical attributes; they could include things like "I love my compassionate nature," or "I love my ability to immediately put other people at ease," or "I love the fact that I have great inner strength." Tape the card to your mirror, computer, refrigerator, or other place where you can frequently be reminded of the gifts that are uniquely yours. ☺

11 Notice Synchronicity

When coincidence shows up in your life, bringing you just what you wanted, you might shrug it off as one of those once-in-a-lifetime incidents. But begin to notice how frequently it happens and feel joyful when it does because you are attracting synchronicity into your life. When you desire, for example, to fall in love with a gorgeous guy and suddenly he shows up sending you a "wink" or greeting on your online dating site, consider becoming his pen pal. You never know what could develop. The more you notice such synchronistical events, the more you embrace and encourage them, the more they will happen. Feel happy and expectant when they do. ☺

12   Soak in a Scented Bath Amid Orchids

You don't need a reason to indulge in some sensual pleasure. Fill your bathroom with blooming orchids for a super sensual feast for the eyes. Orchids such as oncidiums, cymbidiums, dendrobiums, and paphiopedilums are known for their lush and colorful blooms that can last for weeks. All they need is a little light, warmth, and moisture (bathrooms are perfect places for them). Stick them in antique urns, glazed pottery, or terra-cotta pots. Group them along the window sill, on jardinière shelves, or around a Victorian plant stand. Put on some music. Draw a bath. Drop in your favorite scented oil and a few exquisite orchid blooms. On a bathtub tray or a small table nearby, place a flute filled with sparkling apple cider or champagne, a chocolate truffle, a scented candle, and even a book that inspires you. Take your time, luxuriate, and let the cares and concerns of your day float way. Permit your mind to fill with peaceful, joyful thoughts. When you step out of the bath and back into your world, you will feel renewed and ready to meet whatever challenges may be coming your way ☺

Indulge in Moments of Relaxation

 ### Retreat Within to Clear Your Mind

Your bookshelves need dusting, the dishes still stand in the sink, the floor needs mopping, and you haven't even gotten around to the laundry, but you need a moment to deflect or discharge the worries of the day. Take that time to indulge in something that makes you feel peaceful and relaxed. For example, sit in a rocker and gaze at the fresh red tulips on the kitchen counter. Walk into your garden and inspect your plants for new green shoots. Drop some bread crumbs for the pigeons and mourning doves or fill the birdfeeder with Niger seed for the little yellow finches. Feel the wind on your face, the sun on your back, and freshness of a new moment imbued with tranquility. ☺

Plan a little time off just for yourself to do some inner reflection. The amount of time is not as important as getting the respite you need. Make your time away a priority. It's a small amount of time just for you to clear your head, gather your energy, and get perspective. Retreat to someplace peaceful where you can relax and have a break from the responsibilities of work and family. Don't know of any great retreat places? Take your favorite book and head to a beach. If there's no ocean in your backyard, find a shady bank along the edge of a lake, creek, river, or a pond—someplace where the earth and water meet. Sink into your beach chair, tune into the sounds of nature, open your book, and lose yourself in story. Or, just sit back, close your eyes, and let your mind wander. You don't have to do anything while on your retreat but to make a space for tranquility and joy to fill you. ☺

15 Nourish Your Inner Being

Nourish your inner being by diving into meditative reflection, centering and grounding yourself, and endeavoring to deepen the experience. According to Harvard scientist Herbert Benson, who has conducted studies on Buddhist meditation and the effects of the mind on the body, when you turn inward through meditation, complex activity in the brain (as seen on MRI brain scans) takes place. That activity actually calms the body, reduces stress levels, and promotes healing. Eventually a period of quietude is reached and as your concentration deepens, you experience a disconnect between the body and mind. Some people describe that experience as one of awesome peace and joy. ☺

 ## 16 Memorize a Funny Joke and Share It

Heard any good jokes lately? Have you tried passing them on? Telling a funny joke is a terrific way to cheer up others, defuse tense situations, add much-needed levity in times of stress, and generate some positive effects on your health. Memorizing a joke and telling it to others is just one way to cultivate a sense of humor. Did you know that laughing may actually reduce your risk for heart disease and can mitigate damage incurred when you are experiencing deep distress and pain? Also, some sources say that while sniffles, sneezes, and coughing are contagious, laughter is more so. Want to feel good? Be able to laugh at stressful situations. Did you hear the one about . . . ? ☺

17   Get a Warm Rose Oil Massage

A massage is a great way to release the stress and tension you hold in your body. There's nothing comparable to human touch coupled with aromatherapy to transport you into a place of relaxation and peace. If you don't like rose scent, ask the masseuse to use sandalwood, ylang ylang, myrrh, or your favorite essential oil. Massages are de rigeur at day spas. They are also offered at deeply discounted rates at local colleges with massage therapy training programs. Another option is to ask your significant other to give you a massage, but be advised that making that choice could lead to other activities. Ah, but that could also relieve stress and put a smile on your face. ☺

18   Cook Your Favorite Dish for Yourself

Cook up something spectacular such as the comfort food of your childhood, an exotic creation you first tasted on your honeymoon, or even a savory palate-pleaser you learned to cook when you were dating that foreign guy or girl. If you are a working parent, then it's unlikely you ever cook just to please yourself. So once in a while, cook what you want to eat instead of only what the kids will eat. They can nibble on pizza, ordered in, while you happily savor every bite of that Moroccan tangine chicken, New England crab cakes, Midwestern meatloaf, Southern fried chicken, or other favorite. You know how happy you feel eating your favorite food. That's why it's your favorite. ☺

19   Release the Past and Appreciate the Present

You can never go back to previous moments or past events. Once you have moved through them, they are forever gone. Whatever is in the past that haunts you or makes you sad or fearful necessarily stays there. It cannot be undone. If some past event or encounter still bothers you, do what you can to process through it and let it go. You alone give it the power it has over you. Release it and instead focus on the present moment. Be mindful right now of where you are, who you are, and what you are doing. Paying attention to and being fully present in each moment of your life means you truly will be "showing up for your life." That is the way to happiness. ☺

20   Put a Bamboo Plant in Your Kitchen

Put a lucky bamboo plant on your kitchen counter where it will happily enjoy some warmth. Even if you don't have a green thumb, you can successfully grow this plant. It doesn't need much light and will thrive in water (as long as the water is clean and kept at the same level). According to the ancient Chinese tradition of feng shui, the lucky bamboo (not a bamboo at all but a member of the Dracaena family) creates harmony wherever it is placed. Its numerous long green leaves grow out of a single stalk. If you work from home, put a six-stalk plant in your office to attract prosperity or a three-stalk plant in the bedroom to ensure longevity, wealth, and happiness. ☺

CHAPTER 2

Seek Meaning and Purpose to Have a Happy Life

21 Attend at Least One Religious Service This Week

Participate in your religious or spiritual faith and attend a service this week. Even in our materialistic, consumer-driven society, you can live a purpose-ful, self-actualized, meaningful, and happy life. Research suggests that participation and belief in a religious faith or spiritual tradition is an important ingredient for having that kind of life. One way to stay in touch with your core spiritual beliefs is to regularly attend a religious service or a gathering in which your faith and belief is shared. Some studies link such regular participation to a greater sense of well-being, a stronger connection to community, reinforcement of your beliefs, and a more stable, healthier, and happier family life. If you don't have a specific faith, create a regular ritual to honor what you believe in. It can be an elaborate affair or as simple as finding a few minutes to read about or reflect upon beliefs you find inspiring. ☺

22 Recite a Prayer or Make Up Your Own

Prayer can center you when things are going right in your life, give solace and lift you when you feel down, and remind you that you aren't alone. Praying can help you move forward when you feel stuck or provide hope when you need healing. Harold Koenig, MD, associate professor of psychiatry and medicine at Duke University School of Medicine in Durham, North Carolina, has observed that religious people tend to have healthier lives. Better health means you are more likely to feel greater satisfaction with your life. Recite a prayer that gives you comfort. Or, if you prefer you can make up your own

Seek Meaning and Purpose to Have a Happy Life

prayer. A simple "thank you" is a powerful prayer of gratitude. "I need your help" or "Please guide me" are also excellent points of departure into prayer. Pray and then be still like an empty vessel waiting to be filled. Gratefully receive whatever inspiration, answers, relief, peace, joy, and bliss may come. ☺

23 Read a Book about a Religion That's Unfamiliar

If your heart feels bereft of some spiritual inspiration, explore your options and read a book that focuses on one of the great yet unfamiliar religious traditions of the world. Choose an inspirational book if you need a little lift and encouragement. Read the history of your chosen religion or spiritual tradition if you prefer a historical perspective. Study the sacred texts, for example, the Bible, the Torah, the Koran, and the Vedas. Read biographies of

saints. Let the words and deeds of holy beings such as the Sufi mystic Rumi or the Indian saint Mirabai, who were drunk with love for the Divine, lead you back to your spiritual center where your heart can feel happy again. ☺

24 Designate One Corner of Your Home as Sacred Space

Create an area in your home that can serve as a sanctuary for yoga, prayer, writing in your journal, sipping tea, reading, and reflecting. Make your sacred space private. Add a screen, a large plant, a curtain, or something that defines and separates that space from the rest of the house. Add a small table to hold your spiritual texts, sacred objects, candles, incense, holy oil, or prayer beads. A window or door with a view of a lake or garden is an added bonus. Otherwise hang a piece of silk, a batik, or spiritual art. Regularly retreat to your sanctuary to reconnect with your own inner joy. ☺

25 Memorize a Prayer, Affirmation, or Piece of Spiritual Writing

Not only is it good for your brain, but memorization of a prayer, affirmation, or a piece of profound spiritual writing can provide solace and comfort in times of crisis or deep emotional distress and give you peace. If you were a Christian growing up in America, you may have been expected to memorize the Lord's Prayer, one or more of the psalms or proverbs, or New Testament verses. In other religious traditions, too, there are prayers and religious texts, mantras, and sacred verses that followers can memorize. So close your eyes, open your heart, and mentally recite your favorite affirmation or prayer. Let the words lead you to tranquility and bliss. ☺

26 Become More Tolerant

When was the last time you tried to understand a bias you hold toward something or someone? If it's been a while, now might be the right time to revisit your beliefs. Growing up, many people consciously and unconsciously absorb the biases of their family members, associates, friends, and peers. When you let go of intolerant biases and recognize and respect the beliefs of others, you are practicing tolerance. Consider one or more of the beliefs you still hold. Perhaps your beloved grandmother told you that things would never change or the father you respected taught you not to trust anyone who didn't look or talk like you. Think for yourself. Using truth and fact, compassion and understanding, create a new lens for seeing bias. Visit *www.tolerance.org.* ☺

Seek Meaning and Purpose to Have a Happy Life

27 Practice a Random Act of Kindness Every Day

Push the buttons in the elevator for a fellow rider. Help an elderly person up the steps of a building, a subway exit, or onto a bus. Pick up an item that someone drops. Put your pocket change into a charity box. Invite a fellow shopper to move ahead of you in the check-out line. Shovel the snow off your neighbor's walk. Offer to let someone share your umbrella. Random acts of kindness require very little effort but pay great dividends in the good karma and personal happiness they generate. ☺

 28 Make a Ten-Point List of What's Really Important to You

Millions of people live their lives without a sense of direction. Unless you know what is really important to you and what you want out of life, how are you going to know where you are going, how to get what you want, and what your life purpose is? Think of ten things that are really important to you, for example, family unity. Then make each item as specific as possible. Instead of family unity, maybe you really mean eating meals together, working on the chores together, or praying together. Refine the ten things on your list until you know exactly what is of primary importance to you. These are the things that will make you happiest. Knowing what they are can help you make better choices in your personal life journey. ☺

29 Take a Class to Learn CPR and the Heimlich Maneuver

Imagine the happiness you would feel if you were personally able to save someone's life. Prepare by learning how to do some simple first-aid, cardiopulmonary resuscitation (CPR), and the Heimlich maneuver. Classes are offered through the American Heart Association, the parks and recreation departments of many cities, and also through local hospitals and clinics in community outreach programs. Find a class near you and take it. Then if you witness someone who has a medical emergency, call 911. But also don't hesitate to apply what you have learned. Doing something is better than doing nothing. You may even save someone's life through quick action. Now that's something to be truly happy about. ☺

30 Donate Your Blood Annually on Your Birthday

The greatest gift you can give anyone is the gift of life. Hospitals nationwide provide life-saving blood transfusions every day. Yet, all too often, a shortage of blood prompts blood donation centers, the American Red Cross, and hospitals to call upon citizens to donate and help replenish the nation's blood supply. Blood banks repeatedly call upon their good donors, those who don't mind coming in as frequently as every six weeks, to help them out. Consider donating on a regular basis or even just once a year on your birthday so that someone ill can make it to his or her next birthday. The happiness you feel on your special day thus can be magnified by your generosity. ☺

Seek Meaning and Purpose to Have a Happy Life

31 Call Your Favorite Charity and Offer to Help

Want to live a more virtuous life, but you're not the type to do spontaneous acts of kindness and generosity? Then think of your favorite charitable cause, put together a list of charities that work on behalf of that cause, and call to offer what resources you can to help its work. Few charitable organizations would turn away a volunteer. On the contrary, charities generally need people willing to donate their time and expertise. You can live your life focused on yourself or you can choose the higher path and offer part of your life in work for the betterment of others less fortunate. When performing everyday charitable acts, your life takes on meaning and purpose. ☺

 32 Let the DMV Know You Want to Be an Organ Donor

You won't be using your body after it's breathed its last breath, so why not save someone's life through donation of your vital organs? How about giving a blind person the gift of sight or a burn patient tissue? You can sign up with the organ registry of your state and by letting the Department of Motor Vehicles know your wishes the next time you renew your license. Registering to be an organ donor is easy and can make a huge difference for an individual fighting for life as well as that person's family. Even though organ donation has long been a taboo topic for cultural and religious reasons, most of the world's great religious traditions accept it. Live happier knowing that at your life's end, the organs you no longer need can give someone else a fighting chance to live. ☺

33 Give a Box of Fruit from Your Trees to a Local Food Bank

Pick ripe fruit off your backyard trees and box it up for a local food bank to give to the poor. Giving your surplus fruit and produce to a food bank like Second Harvest will help feed people without resources or options to purchase everything they need. You'll be glad to know you did something nice for someone else and that the excess fruit and vegetables won't be wasted. Even if you live in a city and don't have fruit trees, you could have a small garden and share vegetables and herbs from it with the poor. ☺

34 Create a New Tradition with Your Family

Brainstorm with your children and spouse about making a new family tradition. Perhaps something wonderful and spontaneous occurred as you were preparing to leave for summer vacation, the night before Thanksgiving, the afternoon of the first snowfall, or on the way to the pumpkin patch. Or, maybe you had a pillow fight that ended with everyone making popcorn, S'mores, and watching old movies in their pajamas . . . if it still evokes powerful memories for all of you, make it a tradition. Other ideas might include an annual family cleaning day (when everyone pitches in to tackle the mess in the garage, basement, or attic), an annual family fun day (let a child choose what the family does for the day, even if it's bug hunting), or an annual plant-a-garden day. According to Dr. G. Scott Wooding, best-selling author and leading Canadian authority on parenting teenagers, traditions help to determine family boundaries and help children feel more secure by giving them a sense of belonging to a clearly defined unit. ☺

Write a Mission Statement for Your Life

Your mission statement is a blueprint of your vision for your life. When thinking about writing a mission statement, be specific. If you want to have a happy, meaningful life, ask yourself what actions you will need to take and what values and purposes you must have to drive those actions. What is your raison d'être? What is the focus of your life's work? How do the things you do and the way you treat your family and other people reflect your core values? Maybe you prefer to react as life comes at you. But if not, clarify what you want to do with your life. What will give you lasting peace and happiness, when, at the end of your life, you look back at how you lived? ☺

 ## Call the Police When You Have Witnessed a Crime

Don't turn a blind eye or deaf ear to criminal activity or injustice. Stand up for what is right. If you witness an accident, a robbery, abuse of a child (even if it appears the abuser is the parent), dial 911. Fear of reprisal or worry that getting involved may eat up too much of your time or cause you stress seems trivial when you consider that the crime could happen to a member of your family. You'd want others to help, especially if they witnessed what had transpired. Aid someone in distress. Helping another can be gratifying, and even make you happy, whereas doing nothing can cause feelings of guilt and remorse. ☺

37 Join the Sierra Club or Rainforest Action Network

One way to make your life more meaningful is to join others in working to save the planet. Sometimes things can be accomplished only when working in concert with other like-minded individuals in groups like the Sierra Club or the Rainforest Action Network. Joining a group of people who share your feelings about a common cause can inspire you to do things you might never do on your own. Plus, there is truth to the saying that there's strength in numbers. Although one person working alone may not be able to save a rainforest, thousands or millions of people rallying around a single goal might just accomplish it. ☺

38 Join Amnesty International

Join others who want to make their lives count for the greater good. One way to find meaning in your life is by devoting time, money, and expertise to the fight for others who have been unjustly imprisoned. Their voices have been silenced. Amnesty International works hard to expose such human rights abuses. The organization and its supporters have helped save the lives of thousands of victims of torture and execution at the hands of rogue warlords, armed guerillas, and oppressive regimes and governments. Your help is needed and wanted. Contact *www.amnesty.org/en/how-you-can-help*. ☺

Seek Meaning and Purpose to Have a Happy Life

CHAPTER 3

Attract and Build Happy Relationships

39 List Ten Physical Attributes You Desire in a Mate

If you are unattached and looking for that special someone, this exercise will not only be fun but it could produce exciting results. Law of attraction experts say that when you know exactly what you want, it is easier to attract it. Make a list of the top ten physical attributes you'd like in a potential mate. If you have trouble, close your eyes and visualize this person walking toward you. What does he look like? What does his walk or gait say about him? As he gets closer, can you tell if he is taller than you, the same size, or shorter? If you don't like what you see, change it. Go from general observations to specific until you see him clearly in your mind's eye. Now write down ten specific physical attributes that you want. Be on the lookout for that exact person, now, because your thoughts may be calling him to you. ☺

 ## 40 Research Three Online Dating Sites and Join One

If you feel lonely, do something about it. Visit a few of the online dating sites; read about their audience's demographics and the criteria for joining. Decide on two or three sites that might be a good fit for the type of potential friend or romantic partner you desire. Join one. While dating is still about meeting new people, contemporary dating sites make it easier than ever. You can tell the world exactly what you want: for example, an emotionally healthy individual, a Baby Boomer who loves classic rock n' roll, or someone who loves to pair great cooking with fine wine. So banish those lonesome blues, start tapping those keys to connect with others, and make way for some great camaraderie. With a world of potential new friends at your fingertips, what are you waiting for? ☺

Attract and Build Happy Relationships

Think of Three Topics to Begin a Conversation with a Stranger

Don't worry about becoming tongue-tied around strangers. Think of three things to open a conversation. Can't think of any? Consider remarking on the weather, the facility or environment you share with that person (train station, elevator, grocery store, bank, or airline terminal, for example), or an aspect of her dress or accoutrements. Or comment on a recent news headline. Often, just an opening remark is enough to engage the other person. Make the overture and see where the conversation goes from there. You both may be smiling at each other momentarily. ☺

 ## Flirt with Someone You Meet at the Bookstore

You see a great-looking guy thumbing through a travel guide. Or, maybe he is standing in front of the science fiction, business, or computer bookshelves. The point is that you like what you see. You could walk over, excuse yourself, and reach past him to retrieve the book right in front of him, or, if you are more timid, simply flash a sexy smile after making eye contact. Comment on the book he is reading. Is it a travel guide to Ireland where you once bicycled or saw the Book of Kells? Show curiosity and interest in what he is reading and he might become interested in you. ☺

43 Say Hello to the Person Next to You in the Elevator

Pay attention to the people around you. Instead of standing next to the stranger for the elevator ride up several floors, look her in the eyes and offer a greeting. Hello is easy to say. It's only one word. It might lead into a conversation about the weather, the latest news about your city or town, or something about the environment (the noise next door due to construction, for example). You'll never know where the elevator chit-chat might lead if you don't open your mouth in the first place. And that stranger could become a new friend or romantic interest. ☺

44 Make an Appointment with a Relationship-Issues Expert

When you feel so emotional that you can't think straight, it may be time to seek help. Explain to your partner that you believe the two of you could work through the tough issues if only you could talk about them without pushing each other's buttons. One way to not do that would be to find an impartial third party, perhaps a relationship expert or a marriage and family counselor, to guide you through the emotional minefields. Relationship experts can reveal ways to shift the relationship paradigm so you don't stay in a "stuck" place. Working through the issues can strengthen a relationship and make the individuals feel more hopeful, optimistic, and happier. ☺

Attract and Build Happy Relationships

45 Invite a Friend to a Spa for a Hot Stone Massage

Let your best friend know how much you value her friendship. Invite her for a relaxing afternoon at the spa. Treat her to her favorite relaxation treatment or a hot stone massage. Imagine how great she'll feel when the massage therapist places sanitized warm stones of smooth volcanic rock or basalt on her tired back, shoulders, or neck muscles. If there's been any friction between you, a spa day can ease that as well. So go ahead and book the appointment. Invest the time and cost of the massage in your friendship. A happy relationship with your best friend is worth every penny. ☺

46 Take Your Lover to the Best B&B You Can Afford

Nothing thrives through neglect. That is especially true for romantic relationships. Lavish the kind of attention on your romantic partner that you desire for yourself. Make a reservation at one of the best bed and breakfast establishments in your area. Such accommodations usually offer intimate, cozy settings and comfortable bedrooms (sometimes with fireplaces and Jacuzzi tubs). Breakfasts can range from a simple offering of freshly baked muffins with coffee and juice to an opulent gourmet feast. Surprise your lover with a weekend getaway and watch how love blossoms. ☺

47 Write "I Love You" on a Note and Tuck It Under Your Partner's Pillow

Leave love to its own devices or take some action to evoke a response from your lover. Write a simple "I love you" note and tuck it under your partner's pillow to be found when it's time for bed or after you have already left for the day. Such a simple act will call up strong, loving feelings in him during your absence. Expect a call, possibly the delivery of some flowers, or lots of attention. Want a double dose of happiness? Try it and see for yourself the results. ☺

48 Try Online Dating, Speed Dating, or Matchmakers

Put yourself out there if you haven't dated in a while. Or, if you have and are interested in trying some new ways of meeting interesting people and possibly a life partner, try some of the newest dating strategies. Online dating sites have proliferated in recent years. Some charge a fee and some do not. Increasingly, speed dating is an interesting option utilized by upwardly mobile young professionals. Back in the day, people thought of matchmakers as belonging within only certain cultures, but more recently matchmakers have gone mainstream and have found the Web and the Yellow Pages perfect venues for advertising their services: namely, to help you find Ms. or Mr. Right. If you seek a companion for your life and haven't yet found one that's a keeper, don't give up. You have more options and tools than ever for finding that perfect someone for you. ☺

Attract and Build Happy Relationships

49 Make Sushi with Friends

Host a hands-on, sushi-making party for your friends. Tell each person to invite someone else. You get the supplies (sushi rice, nori or seaweed sheets, crab, cucumber, avocado, and other fillings). Explain the directions: each person puts the rice on the nori, adds the filling she desires, rolls the sheet, wets one end and wraps it over the other to seal close, and then cuts the roll into several pieces. Depending on the number of people participating, you will have plenty of sushi to eat. Sharing a meal with friends is one of the most pleasurable activities known to humankind. And who knows? You just might meet someone special. Saki, anyone? ☺

 ### 50 Write an Invitation to Have Sex and Slide It Under His Wine Glass

Feeling flirtatious and sexy? Are you ready for a romantic tryst? Not yet finished with the wine? Slip a little note under his glass. Invite him to join you for some fun. Don't make it seem like he's expected to perform. Instead, tease, tantalize, and titillate. Let that strap of your little black dress slide off your shoulder. Lean forward and engage his attention. Seduce him. Help him believe that in that moment, he is the only man in the world for you. Hold his hand. Let your mutual arousal build and set the pace for everything else. Who needs another glass of wine? Enjoy. ☺

 ### 51 Tell Her Two Ways to Pleasure You

Most men and women find bring-ing up this topic a little tricky. You know what gives you pleasure. And she knows what she likes. Here's an easy way to enter a discussion about sex. Talk about how the ancients did it. Read the Kama Sutra or a book about Tantric yoga practices that utilize the sexual act as a means to enlightenment. Read about the practices of the ancient Greeks and Romans or the erotic exploits of the Victorians (some of them weren't as prudish about sex as you might think). The point is to go from general to specific. Of course, if you are already "performing," you could whisper in her ear how you'd like to be pleasured. Don't forget to ask her what she likes. That way, you'll both be breathlessly happy. ☺

 Serve Your Spouse a Candlelight Supper in Bed

Ever think about what kinds of meals lend themselves to supper in bed? Hot quiche and salad, soup and sandwich, or a casserole with hot popovers or dinner rolls are easy and can be prepared ahead of time. One of the most unexpected yet sweetest things you can do for your significant other is to bring him a luscious meal in bed. You could even share it with him. While he's munching on that delicious meal you made, you can nibble on his shoulder and whisper sweet words of love in his ear. ☺

53 **Establish Personal Boundaries by Saying, "No, It's Not Possible"**

Sometimes the answer is a simple no, especially when you are trying to hold firm a boundary that someone is trying to push across. If you have a hard time saying no, try this exercise. Stand in front of a mirror and practice saying, "No, it's not possible. It's just not possible," then turn and walk away. Think of how wonderful you will feel to be empowered to say yes and no when it suits you. You never again have to give in when you know you don't want to or it is not a good idea. Practice until saying no is as easy as saying yes. And that is a powerful tool in your game-of-life chest. ☺

 ## Be the Kind of Friend You Want to Attract

If you are seeking loyalty and trust in your friendships or the romantic relationship you hope to have, first cultivate those qualities within yourself and then demonstrate them to others. In so doing, you become a magnet for exactly what you want. Similarly, if you seek a gentle, loving spirit for a life partner, avoid someone with a mercurial, volatile, and temperamental nature. Although opposites do sometimes attract, you'll most likely be happiest with a kindred spirit. ☺

 ## Invite a Neighbor over for Coffee and Strudel

Get to know your neighbors. When you meet a neighbor while out tending your flowers, picking up the paper, or walking the dog, say hello to her. Invite her over for coffee and strudel or cinnamon rolls. Get to know her. That means finding out what is important to her, what her hobbies are, what kind of work she does. Find out what mutual interests you share. From that beginning, build friendships with your neighbors. Plan parties on your street for Christmas or Independence Day that involve all the neighbors and their children. You'll be creating memories and cultivating relationships to last a lifetime. ☺

56 Repeat Your Friend's Words Back to Him

The art of actively listening means to be totally engaged when someone is talking to you. When you truly make an effort to understand others, they appreciate it. Consequently, your relationships with them are strengthened. Make sure you truly understand what your friend tells you by repeating his words back to him. You could start with, "I want to make sure I understand what you're telling me." Express your understanding of what he's saying and if it isn't right, he'll correct you. Listen without judging. Be fully present. Pay attention. Your relationships will be stronger and happier as a result of your effort. ☺

CHAPTER 4

Build a Strong and Happy Family

57 Learn How to Be a Better Parent

If you want to be the best parent you can be, sign up for a parenting class. Such classes often can be found through parent teacher organizations, local adult education courses, the family court system, and even online. Learn what to expect from your child as he or she goes through various stages to adulthood. Discover techniques for discipline that do not involve yelling, spanking, screaming, or arguing. Understand why children need boundaries and guidelines as they grow. Invest a little time in becoming a better parent if you want to raise strong, self-sufficient, well-adjusted, happy children. ☺

58 Lavishly Praise Behavior You Want Repeated

It's human nature to repeat behaviors that get a lot of attention. When it comes to your efforts to build a strong, happy family, the key is to focus on the positive behaviors you want repeated and not the negative ones. Try also to lavish praise consistently for that particular behavior. What do you do when the behavior is bad? You ignore what you can. Refuse to give it any attention. And pick your fights carefully. Because attention is usually what the other individual or child is seeking. Your attention is the payoff for her acting out or doing something praiseworthy. So praise what you like, and ignore, if you can, what you don't like. ☺

Build a Strong and Happy Family

59 ## Help Children Understand Why Grandparents Are Family Treasures

If your children have grown up with grandparents around, they are truly lucky. Grandparents are repositories of memories and details of a bygone era and as such are often treasure troves of information for younger generations. Encourage lively discourse between the older and younger generations of your family. Teach your children why their grandparents are so special. Encourage them to do an oral history project, interviewing their grandparents for true stories about growing up in a different time (and possibly place) in the world. ☺

60 ## Pay an Allowance Appropriate for Your Child's Age

Assign age-appropriate chores for your children and reward them with a regular allowance. Although some financial experts say not to link chores to an allowance, many parents do. Earning allowances through work instills in the child a sense of responsibility, accountability, self-discipline, and pride for work well done. Allowances are also a great way to teach your children about money management. Give them the option of earning extra money for special projects. Teach your children how to wisely spend, save, and, depending on their age, invest. When it is their own money they must spend for the things they want, chances are they will learn to make better-informed purchasing decisions. And you will feel happier when your children are no longer treating you like you're the bank. ☺

61 Assign Each Family Member a Night to Plan and Cook Dinner

Ever too tired to cook? Encourage each family member to choose one day each week to prepare the family meal. Be graceful and supportive if you're presented with a stack of peanut butter and jelly sandwiches. Get children an age-appropriate cookbook and help them make some recipes. After that, they will be on their own. Even little children as young as four or five can prepare food. Show them how to wash berries and grapes and break off pieces of bananas, and then demonstrate how to stir in some fruit yogurt as salad dressing. Train the whole family so that the next time you are too tired to cook, you can relax and check the family schedule to see who's turn it is to cook. ☺

62 Schedule a Family Meeting Each Week to Air Grievances

Let each person in your family know that you care about the problems he faces and the issues he may have with you or other family members. Set aside time each week to air family grievances. Avoid allocating blame and instead identify the problem and encourage discussion aimed at finding possible solutions. There may be solutions that require sacrifices to be made by the individuals involved in the conflict. For example, a fight between siblings over a last piece of cake might necessitate dividing the slice between the two children so each gets less but both get some. By airing grievances and discussing options, you will be demonstrating conflict resolution skills—a great real-life tool for your children and other family members to have. ☺

Build a Strong and Happy Family

63 Learn Three Conflict Resolution Techniques and Use Them Regularly

Three basic mechanisms for dealing with conflict are avoidance, accommodation, and collaboration. Use conflict resolution techniques on a regular basis when you are dealing with family conflicts and disagreements. For example, when you are putting masking tape on the floor of the family room in order to separate your children from each other because you can't stand their incessant arguing, do so with a calm, thoughtful, and respectful demeanor. Show them what courtesy, kindness, empathy, and understanding look like. Listen to both sides and demonstrate your desire for a constructive solution. It may be necessary to restate their problem, paraphrasing it in your own words so both of them are satisfied that you truly

understand. Impress upon both children your desire that a solution be found. At all times, speak calmly and avoid being confrontational and aggressive. When the optimal solution is found, happiness and peace will again prevail. ☺

64 Write a Succinct Message Clarifying Your Point

The next time your spouse turns a deaf ear to your point of view, try a new strategy. Write her a succinctly worded note. Resist the urge to call her names, to point out her stubborn streak, or threaten her. Instead, create a lens for her to see your position on the subject. Argue your point without finding fault with her as a person. Show respect for her view, but reveal why you've arrived at the opposite conclusion. She's not your enemy. Tackle the problem, not her, and you may find that she isn't all that attached to her point of view after all. Apply the same strategy to talking with her and you may even find her listening. ☺

65 Copy a Treasured Family Recipe for Relatives

Strengthen your family connections by reaching out to your relatives wherever they may be. One way to forge a stronger family identity is to host a picnic reunion and invite all your relatives. Make a special dish from a recipe handed down from previous generations. Before the day is over, make certain that each family gets a copy of that treasured recipe. Encourage them to pass it along to their children and grandchildren. Your effort creates a tangible link to the past, encourages a celebration of your shared identity, calls up memories of past eras and perhaps historical events, and strengthens family bonds. Those beloved

relatives who made that dish perhaps even centuries before you have long since passed on, but you can remember them whenever you make it. ☺

66 Schedule One Hour after Dinner to Do Crafts with the Kids

After the dishes are done and the homework has been put away, turn off the television and turn on your creativity. Get out the craft box and create something fun, whimsical, or beautiful with the kids. Quality time with your children is never time wasted. They need time with you to feel loved and wanted. Instead of allowing them to sit in front of the television and get bombarded with undesirable messages, establish an hour of family fellowship and watch them thrive. ☺

Build a Strong and Happy Family

Play Soccer or Other Outdoor Activities with Your Family

When your children are old enough to run around, get out a soccer ball and take it to the yard or park. Children love to participate in activities with their parents. Whether or not you realize it, you are teaching your child even as you play games with him. As you demonstrate a competitive spirit, team cooperation, respect for the rules of the game, and good sportsmanship whether you win or lose, he learns through observation, listening, and participation. So go outside and run around with your kids. If soccer isn't your thing, make up a game. The point is to play, set a good example, and have fun with the little (or not so little) ones in your life. ☺

68 Make a Birthday Card Instead of Buying One

Get the whole family involved in making a card for that special birthday gal. A sheet or two of colored paper, paste, scissors, colored pens, and some magazines are all you need to make a great, personalized birthday card guaranteed to evoke smiles of appreciation. Find birthday greetings on the Internet or make up your own. Use the magazines for images or words. You may decide that making a card that says exactly what you want is way more fun than perusing dozens of cards on a store shelf. Oh, and since it costs nothing when you already have the materials on hand, you've got another reason to smile. ☺

69 Choose Two Days a Month to Play Board Games with Your Family

Spend time with your family playing board games or other types of fun activities that stimulate your children's imaginations. Many studies support the premise that children thrive when they are in a family that spends quality time together. Their bonds to each other and their parents are strengthened as well as their sense of identity and belonging. And you may find that you enjoy the time together just as much as they do. It's just another way to build happy relationships. ☺

70 Set and Enforce an Age-Appropriate Curfew for Your Child

Have a family meeting to discuss the reasons for establishing a curfew. Explain to your teen that

his life may depend on honoring that curfew. Many American cities and town have legislated curfew times for teens. For example, some communities have established a 6 P.M. weekend curfew for teens without an adult chaperone. Other cities have partnered with parents to have law enforcement return teens to their homes if caught out and about after curfew and before 6 a.m. A curfew can allow you to rest easier knowing that your responsible teen will be home by a certain time. ☺

71 Create a Multigenerational Scrapbook Detailing Your Family History

Are you the keeper of family photos? Why not create a scrapbook with your children and spouse to trace your family's lineage and document births, deaths, marriages, and other important

Build a Strong and Happy Family

events? During this process, you can teach your children about their ancestry, perhaps inspire one of them to write a report on a famous ancestor, or learn about vital health history. A scrapbook can contain pages with old letters, documents, deeds, and other keepsake documents. You'll not only have hours of fun working on it and sharing it with relatives on celebratory occasions and holidays, you'll feel a sense of pride and joy at knowing the details of your family's lineage. ☺

When were you born? What town, village, or city? What country? Who were your parents? What kind of work did they do? Then ask open-ended questions. Tell me about your earliest memories? What was life like for you growing up in your town? Ask questions about certain periods in his life such as preadolescent, teen, young adult, middle age, and golden years, for example. Long after he has passed away, you can relive those moments and feel joyful that you took the time to make the video. ☺

72 Make a Video Record of an Elderly Family Member Sharing Memories

Before a parent, grandparent, great aunt, or great uncle gets any older, ask him or her to join you for a videotaped chat. Make it informal and begin with easy questions that can serve as points of departure into his story.

73 Give Ten Minutes of Undivided Attention to Each Family Member

Some days, it seems that everybody is clamoring for your attention. But when it comes to family members, it's important that you give it to them. Ten minutes often is not enough to really get started talking, but it shows your loved ones that you care deeply about what troubles them and that you want to help. Even if your help is just listening to them vent, do it. You can always set aside another ten minutes to continue the discussion at a later time. Consider the alternative. Brushing them aside for more urgent matters sends the wrong signal. Make time for loved ones before they leave your nest. Isn't it true that you are happiest when you know that they are happy too? ☺

 ## 74 Ask Each Child to Make Up a New Game for the Family to Play

Kids are so imaginative that if you give them a big box, some wooden spoons, and a few stuffed animals, they will use the items to create an imaginary world with themselves as characters. Help them turn on their imaginations. Ask each child to make up a new game for the family to play together. If there are too many games for one afternoon or evening, give each child a special night on which her game will be played. Have fun, get into the role that's created for you, giggle along with them, and feel the loving bond between you growing. ☺

CHAPTER 5

Take the Healthy Path to Happiness

Wash Your Hands Often

Good health requires good hygiene. Wash your hands with soap and water or use a hand sanitizer to prevent the spread of germs. It's particularly important to wash your hands before eating and preparing food and before and after inserting contact lenses into your eyes. Also, you should wash your hands after using the toilet, changing the baby's diaper, blowing your nose, handling garbage, touching any animal or animal waste, sneezing or coughing, or using any public restroom. Encourage your family to practice good hygiene along with you. You'll be happier if everyone stays healthy. ☺

 ## Plant a Vegetable Garden and Eat the Produce

You consciously choose to eat healthier, avoid purchasing packaged foods, and buy organic whenever possible. Still, how can you be certain that your food hasn't been treated in some way with agents you want to avoid (such as those that may cause cancer). Try growing your own food. Plant a postage stamp-sized garden and do companion plantings, (that is, placing plants known to repel specific pests next to plants that attract those pests) to keep down the pest population. You don't need much space for a small kitchen garden, but if space is a major consideration, you can grow your veggies in pots and planters on the patio. Freshly picked tomatoes, peppers, and other vegetables taste far superior and have greater nutritional value than their shipped and warehoused counterparts. You'll be happier eating organic food from your garden. ☺

77 Nibble a Piece of Dark Chocolate

When you want a moment of pure pleasure, eat some dark chocolate. Not only does it make you feel good, it has specific health benefits. Dark chocolate is believed to lower high blood pressure, improve blood flow in arteries, and act as a powerful antioxidant. Dark chocolate may function somewhat like low-dose aspirin in reducing the blood's clotting ability, thereby reducing blood clots. Also, it has been shown to reduce the LDL or "bad" cholesterol oxidation. Finally, dark chocolate increases the brain's serotonin and endorphin levels, enhancing feelings of pleasure and happiness. A caveat, however, is that milk seems to block the antioxidant absorption benefit of dark chocolate, and you have to balance the chocolate's calories against the total calories you consume each day. Just nibbling a little can lift your spirits. ☺

 ## 78 Put a Water Fountain in Your Home

Put a water fountain in your home office, entry, or family room to influence the flow of positive energy throughout the house. Consider placing a found or oval fountain in the wealth corner of your home. Check a feng shui bagua chart for optimal placement. The bagua map can be found in nearly every book about feng shui or in Asian import stores. Let the gentle sound of flowing water remind you of the blessings of all kinds of abundance, wealth, and peace flowing into your life. ☺

79 Take Ten-Minute Stretch Breaks Throughout the Day

You know how stiff your body feels when you finally get up out of that chair after hours of crunching numbers, or going through the mail, or staring at the computer screen while trying to make sense of some business project. Think about it A little ache or pain once in a while is one thing, but chronic daily abuse of your body is unhealthy. It takes only a few minutes to stretch. Some stretches can even be done sitting in a chair or standing in front of your desk. If you happen to have a yoga mat, take it with you on your break or lunch hour to a private, peaceful area in your workplace or outside in nature and do some stretches combined with breath work and meditation. You'll feel rejuvenated and centered and your body's flexibility will be restored. ☺

 Try New Positions During Sex

Ever tire of sex the same way? Try some new positions. Experiment imaginatively before, during, and after sex. You can get in plenty of stretches and a decent

cardio workout as well, not to mention all those pleasurable endorphins flowing. If you can't dream up any new ways to turn on, tantalize, and titillate your partner, consider the vast world of positions found in Tantric yoga practice. Read The Kama Sutra or just visit your local bookstore or Amazon.com for books that can provide insights. Put a little sizzle back into your relationship with some imaginative sex. ☺

 Complete a Half-Day Fast for Purification

Check with your physician to ensure that you can safely start a fast. There are many types of fasts, from total abstinence of food to eating only certain types of food or juices. A fast can last for a few hours to a day or more. People who fast usually drink water or juice to keep their bodies properly hydrated. Because so many debilitating diseases are

Take the Healthy Path to Happiness

related to overconsumption of food and diets high in fat, sugar, and other less-than-nutritious ingredients, consider undertaking a fast for detoxification and rejuvenation. As you fast, your body uses its energy to cleanse itself. Many people believe that fasting can make you more energetic, enable you to think more clearly, and increase your sense of well-being and happiness. ☺

 82 Take Five Deep Breaths at Intervals Throughout the Day

Calm the mind by breathing deeply five times from your belly like you naturally did when you were a baby. Stop the mental thought chatter and just "be." Experience the present moment as it eternally renews itself in infinite diversity. To be mindful is to have an awareness of the moment without thinking or talking about it. By slowing the breath and thought, you experience tranquility and happiness. ☺

 83 Avoid Exposure to Toxic Chemicals

Happiness is closely linked to good health, and one way to stay healthy is to avoid exposure to all kinds of toxic agents. Read and follow safe-use labels on all products containing toxins or carcinogenic agents, including those for your garden, lawn, or landscape. You might instead choose pest-resistant plants, pull pest-infected leaves and carefully dispose of them, yank out invasive weeds before they reseed themselves over the yard, and use compost and mulch to create healthy soil. Also, choose less-toxic products such as soaps and herbicidal oils to treat troublesome pest problems. ☺

Join a Softball or Bowling League

Get active and you will feel better. If you prefer team sports to those you do solo, join a softball or bowling team or organize one that includes people from your circle of friends or business colleagues. Softball teams and bowling leagues play other players, so even as you are having fun with friends on your team you are also potentially making new friends with players from other teams. Psychologists say those who live isolated lives or without strong social networks are not as happy as those who have strong bonds, social connections, and ongoing support from friends and family. ☺

 ## Give Up Smoking

Find a way to quit smoking if you want to feel healthier, breathe easier, and reduce the possibility of becoming ill, or are pregnant and want a healthy baby. Saving money is another reason to quit. If you give up a three-packs-a-day habit, you'll save hundreds of dollars each year. Nicotine addiction can wreak havoc on your health, and that will cost you more than a pack of smokes. But quitting will help you heal faster. If you want to quit but haven't been successful, don't give up. Many smokers have had to quit several times before they were successful. You have many options including nicotine nasal sprays and inhalers, several oral drugs, patches, and numerous programs and support groups and services. Talk with your doctor, and learn more at *www.surgeongeneral.gov/tobacco*. ☺

Take the Healthy Path to Happiness

86 Do Physical Exercises in the Park on Saturday Mornings

If you like stretching, walking, or running, do it in nature. Consider joining a group of people who congregate in a nearby park on Saturday morning to practice tai chi, chi gong, or yoga. Doctors say the best kind of exercise is the kind that you enjoy enough to keep doing consistently. If you like to socialize while working out, get out of the house and meet some friends at the high school football field, on a jogging trail, or at a local park. Breathe some fresh air, take in the lovely sights and sounds of nature, and work out while enjoying the camaraderie of others. ☺

87 Eat Nuts, Salmon, and Foods High in Omega-3 Fatty Acids

Even though omega-3 fatty acids are necessary for survival and are especially good for heart and brain health, your body doesn't produce them. You get them in the foods you eat. Consumption of a diet rich in omega-3 fatty acids is good for your heart health, reducing blood pressure and decreasing the risk of clots. Doctors recommend eating two or more servings each week of fish such as halibut, herring, salmon, sardines, snapper, swordfish, and tuna. Also, flaxseeds and walnuts, wheat germ, pumpkin, and spinach are high in omega-3 fatty acids. Medical research has shown that eating walnuts, in particular, can significantly lower the levels of cholesterol in your blood. So, if you want a healthy heart and food for your brain, eat your fish and enjoy snacks of walnuts or almonds. However, snack on nuts in moderation since they are high in calories. ☺

88 Daydream for Twenty Minutes Every Morning

Daydreaming can stimulate your mind in creative ways, reduce stress, elevate your mood, organize your thinking, stimulate ideas for solutions to problems, and help you gain new perspectives on troubling issues. Assuming that you are not using daydreams to escape from being fully engaged in your life or retreating from your responsibilities, then a regular period of daydreaming is not only healthy but helpful in solving problems and fostering creativity. Set a timer. Let your thoughts take flight to a Greek island, a trekking path high in the Himalayas, a manicured estate in England, a beach in Barbados, or some-

where else; indulge yourself. Let your thoughts take flight. ☺

89 Get at Least Eight Hours of Sleep Each Night

If you want to wake up happy with a hopeful, positive outlook, get adequate sleep. Your body needs it. Without sufficient sleep, sleep researchers say, your mental function becomes impaired. Certain regulatory systems and important organs continue their vital work while you sleep. Researchers have been able to pinpoint parts of the brain that actually increase their activities when subjects are asleep. Inadequate sleep has serious consequences. For example, it can negatively impact your daytime performance, causing lower levels of energy and duller thinking. Adequate sleep, however, enables you to wake up refreshed, energized, and in a good mood. ☺

90 ## Do Crossword or Number Puzzles to Keep Your Brain Sharp

Keep your brain fit as you age by stimulating it with memory exercises and problem-solving games. Doing daily crossword or number puzzles means your brain gets a sustained cognitive workout every day. Experts say that such mental aerobics can stave off neurodegenerative diseases, including Alzheimer's. In one study, leisure activities associated with reduced risk of dementia also included reading or playing a musical instrument. A study published in the *New England Journal of Medicine* noted that stimulating and challenging mental activities can build up cognitive reserve. That means as brain cells are lost due to aging, there will be new cells to replace them. ☺

91 ## Take a Spa Day

When you feel like life has become a treadmill and you just need to step off for a respite, treat yourself to a day at the spa. Get a manicure, pedicure, or skin rejuvenation facial. Or, if you'd like to try something a tad more radical, get a colon cleansing, take a mud bath, or slip into a sensory-deprivation tank. For a healthy state of mind and body, try some treatments at an upscale med-spa center that integrates innovative, cutting-edge therapies and holistic healing modalities with ancient practices of other cultures. ☺

 92 ## Go on Vacation Every Year

Take your vacations; they're good for you. One study found that the risk of suffering a fatal heart attack decreased in middle-age men who regularly took an annual vacation. Even so, roughly a third of Americans who have accrued vacation time don't take all of the time they are allotted. Vacations can restore balance between work and the other areas of your life by providing relief from the relentless pressures of work commitments, schedules, and deadlines. A vacation can provide much-needed rest, recovery, and renewal, but vacations can also create stress. Make sure to factor in some vacation days just to hang out, sleep, and rejuvenate yourself if you want to return to work feeling happy and recharged. ☺

CHAPTER 6

Put Your Career on a Happy Track

93 Put into Practice Three to Seven Habits for Success

Motivational speakers will tell you there are a number of good habits that you can implement to aid in your pursuit of success. Start by establishing three new habits and then expand the number to seven or even more. These successful habits might include:

- Learn to manage your time and not waste it.
- Be curious and have a desire to always be learning.
- Practice self-discipline because your motivation and work ethic depend upon it.
- Always follow through and complete what you start.
- Be of service to others.
- Do the right thing; show your integrity.
- Keep your word.

Cultivate a sense of enthusiasm and joy, then notice how you are suddenly attracting exactly the kind of people—helpers, mentors, investors, and guides—you need for success. ☺

94 Create a Time Line and Action List for Starting Your Own Company

You may want to start your own company, but aren't sure when is the best time to launch it—next week, six or seven months from now, five years out? Tasks and time lines often go together. You've heard of the proverbial expression, "getting all your ducks in a row." Ask yourself, what ducks will I need to line up in order to launch? Make a list of specific actions to undertake and items to prepare or acquire. Then plug your list into a calendar and get ready for the launch date. ☺

Put Your Career on a Happy Track

95 Ask a Favorite Boss or Someone You Admire to Mentor You

Having a mentor can put you on a fast track in your job or propel your career into liftoff. Just asking someone to mentor you suggests to others that you are eager to move ahead and that you may even be an overachiever. In fact, if you have a career or job with various aspects that require special skills, why not seek out several mentors, one for each specialized area? Some career strategists believe that mentors are vital if you desire to rise quickly through the ranks. Plus, they can be wonderful allies as you pursue your dreams. A bonus is that both protégés and mentors seem to benefit from such relationships. ☺

96 List Five of Your Guiding Principles

Your guiding principles are those that reflect your core beliefs and guide not only what you do but why and how you do it. Try to list five principles that you use to guide you in your work or career. For example, do you expect others to demonstrate ethical behavior? Do you believe in being open and transparent? How about being flexible, innovative, efficient, and effective? Do you value diversity in your treatment of all people? If your guiding principles and those of your company are in alignment, you are likely to be much happier on the job than if they are in conflict. ☺

97 Spearhead a Pet Project

If there's a project that you are itching to take on, then make it happen. Start with a discussion with a trusted colleague or supervisor who is empowered with the knowledge necessary to limit or expand scope of the project and who knows what is needed to get a go Then dig deep, do the work, write a project proposal, and volunt to oversee it from start to finish. Your passion will be the driving to manifest the project and your creativity and drive will ensure that your managers and bosses take notice. A self-starter with a "can do" attitude is an asset to any company. ☺

98 Think of Two Reasons You Haven't Moved Forward in Your Job

This may seem like an exercise in negative thinking, but it isn't. In fact, it's just the opposite. In order to move forward, you have to know what holds you back and then figure out how to deal with whatever it is. For example, you are always over budget and behind schedule on projects assigned to you. Figure out why that is and what specific steps you can take to ensure it won't happen again. If the problem is lack of knowledge, take some critical education classes, refresher courses, or find other ways to learn more about your field. If you are in a management position and are chronically late to meetings, don't possess great conflict resolution skills, or are not a people person, you may want to consider shifting into a different job. Working on a job that you enjoy will increase your levels of happiness. ☺

99 Create a Chart to Outline the Steps of Your Career

In college, you may have had a clear idea of where you wanted to be three to five years after graduation, but have you considered it since?

Now is as good a time as any to create a chart for your new career goals. Use the chart to outline each step and put a date beside the steps. You may find it easier to work on this by starting with your ultimate goal, say in five years, and then working back to the present. Do this exercise when you don't have other matters clamoring for your time and attention; your career deserves your focused and thoughtful consideration. ☺

 ## 100 Join Toastmasters to Improve Your Oral Communication Skills

You think you've got public speaking at your workplace nailed, but if you have any doubt or believe that there's always room for improvement, seek help from organizations like Toastmasters. Toastmasters International, in particular, has clubs and groups worldwide. You are bound to find one in your area. At meetings you can meet other people like yourself who are interested in being comfortable and capable of speaking spontaneously or doing more formal presentations, but you can also work on other leadership skills such as thinking and listening. Serving on a volunteer basis in a group like Toastmasters can help you learn more about public relations, organizing meetings, running contests, and conducting membership campaigns. Additionally, you'll be meeting people just like yourself who are motivated to succeed in their lives. You might even talk a coworker or two into attending with you. ☺

101 Spend Five Minutes Before Bed Imagining Forthcoming Fame

The work you do is satisfying, but you want recognition for those big accomplishments and milestones. Use the law of attraction to draw to yourself the fame you desire. Before you retire for the night, take five minutes to clear your mind. Focus. Use your imagination to create a scenario in which you are receiving accolades, praise, and ovations by industry leaders, your business colleagues, and others. Now, add your emotion to your imagined scene. Concentrate on your emotional feelings and mood as you listen to the words spoken by others about your achievements and accomplishments. Your subconscious doesn't know real experience from imagined. According to the teachings of the law of attraction, you just have to believe the experience can be yours and supercharge it with emotion in order to manifest it in your life. Let those happy feelings permeate your dream and your time at work. ☺

102 List Five Ways You Provide Value to Your Company

You want a promotion but you believe that management sees you as just another worker bee. It's up to you to convince your superiors otherwise. Make a list of at least five ways the company benefits from your work efforts. For example, does your sense of optimism permeate the workplace, infusing everyone with enthusiasm? Doesn't that positively impact company morale? Are you a great organizer who practices time management techniques so that you tend to be more efficient and productive than others doing the same work? Do you come to brainstorming sessions brimming with new ideas? Are you great at assessing value, doing marketing analysis, or interpreting statistical data? Can others always count on you? Show higher-ups your value to the company and remember that the answer will always be no until you ask for what you want. ☺

103 Summarize Three Points of Your Adversary's Argument

If you really want to understand and overcome an adversary's point of view, actively listen to what she is telling you. Repeat your understanding of what she said (for that tends to reinforce what you thought you heard), and, finally, summarize three points of her position. Only when you fully understand where she's coming from, will you be able to align with her and make your case against her position. Practice that strategy on friends and coworkers during friendly, yet lively, discussions of opposing points of view. Being able to quickly comprehend an opposing viewpoint and then to overcome the objections to your position can greatly benefit your business. ☺

104 Brainstorm Three Ways to be Happier at Work

Think of three things you could do to make yourself happier on the job. Would listening to your favorite music on an MP3 player lift your spirits? Or, could taping some miniature pictures of your family members to the bottom of your computer screen inspire you to be happy? Would checking your e-mail at noon instead of when you first arrive keep your mood elevated throughout the morning? Find ways to be happy while at work and your creativity and productivity are likely to rise along with your mood. ☺

105 De-Stress Before Bed Each Night

After a long day at work, are you tense, tossing and turning while try-ing to go to sleep every night? Release stress before you go to sleep and you may find that you are able to fall asleep more quickly, have a better quality of sleep, and wake up more rested and refreshed. There are myriad ways to calm your mind and let go of the tension held in your body, including taking a warm bath, sipping a glass of wine or warm milk, listening to relaxation tapes or peaceful music, doing some deep breathing, or praying to release concerns to a higher power. Rather than living your life stressed out, make it a point to let go of the tension accumulated throughout the day so that you get deep, restor-ative sleep. ☺

106 Figure Out an Exit Strategy

An important principle taught in most small business entrepreneur classes is the exit strategy. Exit strategies are vital to consider when things are not going the way you expected, whether you anticipate striking out on your own or just leaving your current track. Either way, shifting direction on your career track or deciding to move in a completely different direction necessarily takes some forethought and a plan, especially if you desire to make your move with dignity and grace. Both will be important for your mental and emotional well-being. You don't want your happiness (at leaving or making a lateral move) to hurt or inconvenience someone else if you can avoid it. That's where a well-conceived, well-executed plan can make a huge difference. ☺

107 Safeguard Your Professional Relationships

The old adage about not burning your bridges in case you have to cross them again one day applies to your career: it's not in your best interest to damage or sever professional relationships. You never know when you might meet those individuals again and have to conduct business together. If you are at least on good speaking terms and have shown respect, it will be a lot easier to establish a smooth working relationship. Stay optimistic and do your best to protect and safeguard all professional relationships. That way, you can feel happier and more assured that you are doing something vital to keeping your career or job on track. ☺

 108 Offer to Mentor a New College Grad in Your Career Field

If a new college graduate has just entered the work force after being hired by your company, offer to mentor him. If you are a supervisor or senior-level manager, mentoring a recent college graduate can benefit you both. You can gain an understanding about the business worldview held by him and his peers and also learn what motivates them. On the flip side, you can help him learn about your industry, trade regulations, business relationships, and perhaps help him to rise through the ranks more quickly. It's a win-win for everyone. ☺

109 Subscribe to at Least One Industry Trade Journal

Keep up to date on advances, breakthroughs, and new information about your specific industry by subscribing to at least one trade journal. Trade journals announce industry trade shows, conventions, and often roundtable or networking meetings that you may want to attend in order to stay abreast of the latest developments in your field. In addition, you can gain insights into how to make your business even stronger and more competitive. An added bonus is that you may find people through recruitment ads, blurbs, or hard news stories who might become potential allies or recruits for your company.   ☺

CHAPTER 7

Learn to Be Happy Dealing with Finances

110 Make a Household Budget and Stick to It for at Least a Month

Do you need a plan to get out of debt? When you know where you are going, you can control how you get there. Start by writing down exactly how much money you have coming in each month and the sources of your income streams. List all your bills, starting with those that carry late payment fees or debts with high interest rates. Follow up with another list of your monthly needs. Brainstorm low-cost ways to meet your financial obligations and needs, making your lunch instead of buying it, taking a thermos of coffee and forgoing the cup at the local coffee house, and carpooling instead of driving, for example. Write the due dates of all bills on your calendar. Before you begin writing out checks, first pay yourself a small fixed amount to put into your savings. Live frugally but feel empowered as you watch the debt begin to shrink and your savings begin to grow little by little. ☺

111 Set a Timer for Twenty Minutes and Tackle Your Bills

If you are like many people, you hate paying bills. Yet, you must attend to that dreaded chore to maintain good credit. An excellent way to deal with unpleasant tasks is to tackle them as soon as possible. Procrastinating only invites your stress to increase. But relief comes as soon as the job is done. So gather those bills together, get your calculator, the checkbook, a pen, and set a timer. Hunker down for twenty minutes or until the job is done. Then reward yourself with a glass of wine, a piece of dark chocolate, or anything that makes you happy. ☺

Learn to Be Happy Dealing with Finances

Balance Your Bankbook Every Statement Cycle

If you bank online, you may simply check your balances each day and take note of which bills have been paid or are queued up for payment. However, working with a checkbook helps you know at a glance what your balance is when you are not near a computer. Be diligent about recording any check you write when you are making purchases throughout the day. Some banks send with your monthly statement a how-to guide to balancing your checkbook, and it's worth taking a few moments to stay on top of your balances. When the monthly bank statement arrives and there aren't any scary surprises, you'll feel both relieved and happy. ☺

 ## Close Your Eyes and Imagine that You Are a Magnet for Money

Practitioners of the universal law of attraction say that what you think about most is what you attract into your life. Instead of worrying about money, think of yourself as a money magnet. Yoke your willpower and actions to your positive thinking. Believe that money from various sources (known and unknown) is flowing to you. Don't discount any of the myriad ways it might arrive including checks in the mail, found money, gifts, inheritances, rebates and coupons, refunds, dividends, and donations. ☺

Write Down Your Desired Income and Tape It to Your Computer

Do you dream of making a certain amount of money this year

or next? Write it on a piece of paper and tape it to your computer monitor where you can easily see it. Let it remind you of your desire. Set a goal to bring in that amount. Develop a laser focus. If you don't believe it is possible to generate that income from your job, get a second job. Better still, dream up new ways to create income streams. Could you sell things on eBay like the woman who turned flea market and garage sale finds into products that she resold on eBay to the tune of $3,000 in extra monthly income? You can make it happen. ☺

 115 Form an Investment Club with Friends to Learn about Money

The next time you and your friends bemoan the economy and how difficult it is to stretch a budget, do something constructive. Propose that you all form an investment club. Learn about how to invest in stocks, bonds, mutual funds, and other types of markets to put your money to work earning more money. If you don't have money to work with initially, make imaginary investments until you do. Track each investment made within your group for six months or a year. Have fun while you learn about attracting money, working with your capital, and building your wealth. ☺

116 Pay Off Your Credit Card with the Highest Interest Rate

Most credit card companies assess finance charges when you don't pay off your balance in full every month. If that practice is causing you to sink deeper in debt, start paying off those cards and stop charging on them, if possible. It will take a lot of willpower and perseverance to get credit card debt paid off, but you can do it. Make a list of all your cards, what you owe, and the interest rate on each. Then pick the one with the highest interest rate and pay down that card until you get it paid off. Reward yourself, but for goodness sake, don't charge it. ☺

117 Write a Plan to Get Out of Debt

You're sticking to your budget and now you want to tackle a bigger plan to get out of debt. It takes about three weeks for a new habit to really stick, so allow at least a month for your brain and spending habits to catch up to your new way of dealing with household expenses. Don't let anything keep you from sticking to that new household budget, and resist the urge to buy new things. Remember, the best time for success is when you no longer can stand failure. Figure out a plan of action to take for those moments when temptation beckons and your willpower weakens. Reward yourself for not giving in. Have a small piece of chocolate, take a walk in a flower garden, or check out a book or video from the library to enjoy in a leisure moment. If you can resist temptation once, you can do again. How empowering is that! ☺

118 Skip One Weekly Latte and Put the Money into Savings

How many times a week do you stop for that special large cup of latte? Try this little experiment: Each time during the week that you feel the impulse to have a $5.00 latte at the usual coffee house, put that amount aside. If you've been stopping every day, you are spending $5.00 per day, roughly $25.00 week, or $100 a month. Over a year, that's $5,200.00 that could be earning more money if you put it into an interest-bearing savings account. ☺

 ## 119 Sign Up for a Wealth Seminar

Wealth begins as a state of mind. You must want it and be willing to work toward having it. Even if you don't have any discretionary income to put to work earning money, at least invest some time in a class to begin to learn about how you can build wealth. Some of the wealthiest people in American history were once poor, hard-working immigrants with little to show for their daily endeavors. Many even faced discrimination. But they had big dreams and didn't let their situation stop them from building great wealth. A wealth seminar could be just what you need to get started working on your own stash of cash. ☺

120 Brainstorm and Create Three New Income Streams

Perhaps you enjoy beadwork and make earrings, belt buckles, and pins while watching television at night. Or, you may have a passion for sports collectibles and pour over your binder of cachets in your leisure time. Whatever your interest, passion, or hobby, consider how you could turn it into a stream of income. Could you make something artsy-craftsy to sell at local art and wine festivals, on eBay, or in galleries featuring the work of local artisans? Think of at least three ways to generate income from your knowledge, passion, and expertise. Yes, there may be a learning curve until you are actually doing it, but you're going to love the extra money flowing in. ☺

Put Past Financial Experiences in Perspective

If you are looking for that silver lining in the dark cloud of America's recent economic downturn, try studying what happened to your budget, income, and investments in order to see what you might do differently from now on. The great psychoanalyst Sigmund Freud once remarked that our illusions allow us to enjoy pleasure but when they collide with reality and are dashed to pieces, we have to accept it. Some of the industrial giants who built America suffered financial failures. However, from those failures, they gleaned information to build future financial empires. Dale Carnegie, for example, said that two of the surest stepping-stones to success were discouragement and failure. Use them to your advantage and a happy and prosperous financial future could be yours. ☺

 ## Listen to Audio Books by Financial Experts During Your Commute

What do you do during your commute other than drive? Talk on your cell? Think about your troubles? Curse at the long line of cars ahead or the guy who just cut you off? Do something productive when you are forced to sit in traffic. Buy some audio books about finance. Or choose audio titles in other areas of your business. Maybe there's an industry topic that you want to know more about or a new language you'd like to learn for a new market you want to tap. You have to be on that road twice a day, so instead of letting all that time go to waste, use the time in ways that can return dividends in your career or business. You may find yourself looking forward to that commute. ☺

123 Visit the U.S Mint to See How Money Is Printed

Plan a family vacation around a trip to the U.S. Mint in Washington, DC. The mint oversees the custody and protection of $100 billion of U.S. gold and silver assets. Why not use the occasion as a field trip to learn about the history of the mint, how it produces currency and coinage for commerce, why a mint mistake can get coin collectors salivating, what is a proof set of collectible coins, and how someone can start a coin collection for fun and to learn history. That trip, quite possibly, could be the highlight of your family vacation. ☺

124 Put Your Money to Work for You

When you inherit property, for example, there's inherent temptation to spend money rather than invest it. However, if you don't need that money and can invest it in mutual funds, annuities, real estate income trust (REITS), or other assets, consult a trusted advisor or investment professional for advice on how to put your money to work earning more money for you. Expenditures on luxury items can give you a thrill, but the happiness isn't lasting. Anytime you have discretionary income that isn't earmarked for your personal or family needs, a better approach to spending it on expensive toys is to buy assets that, over time, will put money into your pocket. ☺

125 Keep a Dollar Bill in Your Pocket or Purse at All Times

There's something reassuring about having money in your purse or pants pocket. Think of that dollar as insurance against developing a poverty mentality. Abolish the sense of deficiency

Learn to Be Happy Dealing with Finances

in your life and try to stay focused on the abundance that you want to manifest. You are certainly not broke as long as you have that dollar. Let the dollar lead you into brainstorming ways of creating more dollars. Positive and hopeful thinking and dreaming can get you started. Goals will pull you a little farther along, and creative ingenuity and concrete effort can remove blockages and shift the flow of money into your life. And being able to manifest the money you need replaces your fear and worry with joy and expectation. ☺

126 Make a Money Manifestation Poster

Hung up about money? Get a little crazy. Pull out a piece of paper, some magazines, a pair of scissors, glue, and some colored pens. Go through the magazines, cutting out images of money or words like "millionaire" or "money magnet." Choose visual images of dreams you would like to manifest as you become more prosperous. In the center of your poster, draw a giant dollar sign or stacks of currency or your personal symbol of wealth. Use the colored pens to draw several spokes away from your symbol of wealth. At the end of each spoke draw a circle. In each circle, write a different way to bring in some money, right now or in the near future. Dream it, draw it, do it. ☺

127 Learn How to Create a P&L for Your Own Finances

If you've never produced a personal profit and loss chart, don't sweat it. It's easy to create and useful for preparing your income tax filings. Really, it's about pulling together two columns of numbers: income and expenses. List all your income sources, such as wages, investment dividends, lottery winnings, social security benefits, income tax refunds, or others, and their respective amounts in one column. A second column lists all your expenses with those amounts also allocated. That means money spent for orthodontic braces, medical insurance premiums, and regular medications go under a "Medical" heading. Also include headings such as Auto, Charity, Child Care, Education, Household (mortgage, moving expenses, for example), and others. Knowing the amount of money coming in exceeds the amount being spent for your needs means you most likely will have money left over. Maybe a lot! Now doesn't that make you happy? ☺

128 Consult an Investment Expert to Get Your IRA Growing

Build a little nest egg for yourself. Open a traditional or Roth individual retirement account (IRA) and put the maximum amount that the IRS will allow in the account each year. Do be wise about investing for your retirement. If you don't understand the difference between the two types of IRAs and the investment possibilities for growing your money as well as the tax ramifications, seek the counsel of a trusted financial advisor. It's all part of growing a fatter nest egg so someday you can become a retiree with a lifestyle that you love and can afford. ☺

129 Buy Yourself a Home

Recent changes in the housing market have made it possible for many people to purchase their first home. It's a huge decision and one that requires careful consideration. You may want to consult a trusted

Learn to Be Happy Dealing with Finances

real estate agent or bank loan officer to get all the facts and to help you understand the process. There are many advantages to owning your own home, not the least of which is having a place of belonging where you can build your life and even start your family, if you haven't already. There are tax advantages to owning your own home, and the best news is that there are huge numbers of homes on the market today and many are much more affordable than they were just a year or two ago. If owning your own place will make you happy, now might be the right time to check into it. ☺

CHAPTER 8

Find Moments
of Happiness
in Crisis

130 Release the Tension

You've dealt with crisis. When it concluded, did you breathe a deep sigh of relief? Whether the crisis you faced took hours, days, weeks, or months to resolve, it probably wasn't something that inspired happiness. But that doesn't mean the next time you must deal with a crisis that you can't find a single moment of happiness during the period that the crisis spans. Perhaps it's the moment when finally you can release the tension you've held in your body and mind. Or, maybe it's the moment when you realize the ordeal is finally over and the outcome is better than you thought it would be. Whatever stage of the crisis you find yourself in, seek out that special place inside yourself where you can feel peace and joy at the miracle of being alive and out of harm's way. Breathe deeply. Let go of the tension. Just be present in that moment and stretch it out. ☺

 131 Learn to Adapt to Change in a Crisis

Change is inherent in every crisis, whether personal, societal, environmental, political, global, or some other type. You'll manage the crises of your life better if you learn to not only adapt to change but to search for the gains (rather than the losses) from each one. By focusing on and finding the profit in a crisis, you are more likely to experience positive emotions, such as openness, compassion, love, and hope, and fewer of the negative emotions, such as fear, apprehension, sadness, and anger that accompany many crisis events. ☺

132 Think of One Thing You Can Control

When you feel disempowered and helpless, it is often because you think you have lost control over your life and can see no way out of your dilemma or darkness. The truth is that the only thing you truly have control over is your own thoughts. No one can ever control those but you. To feel empowered again, you must reset your thoughts. Now, think of one thing in your life that you can control. Do you control what you put into your mouth? What about the position you will sleep in? Or, when and where you will sit or stand? Did you know that one of the meanings of control is to restrain or limit something? Restrain your negative, helpless, and disempowered thinking. Shake up your mental energy with a brisk walk in nature or dance along to the rhythm of some upbeat music. Now re-evaluate your life and see the control you already have. No life is static. It just seems that way. Rather, life is dynamic and fluid, so take heart. ☺

133 Mentally Affirm Two Ways Life May Become Better

Your boyfriend walks out on you. Your dog dies. Your new Camry is totaled by a tree limb. Your boss announces layoffs and your name is first on his list. Some days, it seems that nothing goes right. But remember what Alexander Graham Bell said about doors: one closes and another opens but you don't often see those that open because you are staring regretfully for so long at the ones that are closed. Change is certain, and things can and do get better. Think of two ways that change could happen in positive ways for your life. Expect to be happily surprised when you stop staring at the closed doors and see the new ones opening: a new man walks into your life . . . with dogs. Your new job comes with a car. Life is good and you are on top of the world. Relish the thought. ☺

 134 Ask Experts for Opinions But Rely on Your Own Wisdom

Rely on your inner guidance when you are in a seemingly intractable place and need to make an important decision, such as committing a child with extreme special needs to a specialized care facility. You may fear that you can't make that decision. How can you find help? Seek expert opinions, talk to health providers and caregivers, get insights from families in your situation. Go into the darkness, the place of unknowingness, and quiet the chatter in your mind. Be very quiet and receive what the darkness has to offer. Let your thoughts move toward hope,

inspiration, and, finally, to your decision. Once your decision is made, don't second-guess it. Be at peace. ☺

 135 Think of One Thing You Need to Stay Strong and Focused

Think about what you would need to be grounded and focused if a crisis were to show up in your life five minutes from now. What could instantly calm you and help you deal with a rise in possibly negative emotions? Would a whiff of sandalwood help? How about a shot of brandy? Would fingering your prayer beads or finding a place of absolute silence where you could think and pray work best? A crisis can arise suddenly and without warning. Whether it's an emergency, a cataclysmic natural disaster, or a financial catastrophe, a crisis often requires you to figure something out fairly quickly. Knowing what will get you through the next minute and the minute after that can be as helpful as having an escape plan for the unlikely event that your house catches on fire. ☺

136 Scream into a Pillow

If you are ever so overcome with emotion that you can't seem to hold it inside, scream into a pillow. This technique releases the pent-up energy holding those negative feelings inside and works especially well for anger or grief. Sob your sorrow into the pillow. Or, scream the words of anger that you can no longer hold in. Empty out the feelings. If necessary, pound the pillow with your fists. You may need to get a bigger pillow or even a new one if your beating destroys it. It's a small price to pay for expressing rage. Repeat the process until you know the emotion is spent and there's no longer a need to

do anything. Then, when your peace is restored, do something to make yourself happy like listening to beautiful music or sipping your favorite tea. ☺

137 Skim Pebbles Across Water

At some point when you are in crisis mode, you need to feel expansive and push away the walls of your crucible. When you can steal ten to twenty minutes, retreat into nature and do something mindless, like skimming pebbles across water in a reservoir, lake, river, pond, or sea. If your thoughts start to plow that same old field of concern about the crisis you are facing, sink into an awareness of only your breath. Be mindful of the cycle of inhaling and exhaling. Then, if you can, guide your awareness into the space between breaths. Experience the limitless boundary of your mind and return to serenity. ☺

138 Ignore Melodramatic Rhetoric

You know a drama queen when you see one. Understandably, people in crisis react differently but drama queens are all about being the center of attention. Calm, clear thinking is what is most needed in dealing with a crisis; melodramatic or emotionally inflammatory rhetoric is not helpful. If Chicken Little runs to you and shrieks that the sky is falling and everyone is going to perish, he is either genuinely panicked or vying for attention. One way to deal with him is to not react. Reassure him in a calm, quiet, unfazed tone: "I can see that you are upset. I assure you the sky is not falling. You are overreacting." Let your quiet demeanor and words stand in stark contrast to his prostrations. If he continues, leave the room and reclaim your mental/emotional equilibrium. Don't give away your power to have happiness. ☺

 139 Drink Fresh Juice

Can you say antioxidants? During a crisis, your body responds by releasing turbo-charging stress hormones that flood your cardiovascular system to prepare you to deal with the emergency. But stress hormones flooding the system can also cause damage. Antioxidants, substances found in certain fruits and vegetables, act as scavengers of free radicals (by-products created when cells use oxygen) and can both prevent and repair free radical damage. Squeeze or use a juicer to extract the juice from organic vegetables and fruits such as oranges, lime, strawberries, carrots, apricots, peaches, cantaloupes, and green leafy vegetables. Pomegranate, purple grapes, and cranberries are high in phytochemicals and are good antioxidant agents as well. Drinking fresh, organic juice is especially good for when you are under duress. ☺

140 Take a Sauna or Steam Bath

If you believe that time spent in a sauna or steam bath is healthy because sweating releases unwanted material from the body and improves circulation, you are correct. Make sure that you are in good health by checking with your physician before stepping into a sauna or steam room. Also, it's important to drink lots of water to replace what you lose from perspiration. Taking a sauna or steam bath can eliminate toxins and excess sodium, relax tense and sore muscles, and enable you to relax into your happy place. ☺

141 Read a Passage in an Inspirational Text

What kind of crisis are you facing—financial, medical or health, spiritual, educational, or relationship? Whatever it is, you can bet that others have faced similar situations. Life beats up on everyone from time to time. If you don't want to reach out to a trusted friend or professional, find hope, optimism, and perhaps a path out of your situation in the stories of others. For example, if your spouse needs an organ transplant, read the stories of patients who have already been through that ordeal. Draw inspiration, relief, hope, and a sense of renewal from your reading. ☺

142 Snuggle with Your Favorite Pillow or Blanket

If you are like many people, as a child you had a little pillow or a security blanket that got you through the night. As an adult facing crisis, you may wish you had something tangible like that to give you comfort. If you don't have a favorite blanket or pillow, get yourself over to the linen closet and see if there's a comfy throw, a worn afghan, or a silky coverlet that you could use. Or go to the clearance table at your local department store and pick something out that could become a favorite security blanket. As a child, you loved your blankey because it was yours and only yours. It had your scent on it. You knew what it felt and looked like even with your eyes closed. In times of crisis, seek comfort in what's familiar and makes you feel safe. Wrap yourself in your blanket and let your inner child feel safe again and comforted. ☺

143 Have a Glass of Wine at the End of a Difficult Period

Unwind with a glass of your favorite wine at the end of an exhausting day or difficult period.According to a number of research findings, wine is good for you if you drink it in moderation and as part of a healthy diet. Wine has nonalcoholic phytochemicals (flavanoids and resveratrol) that prevent free radical molecules from damaging your body's cells. Studies show that wine reduces the risk of getting certain cancers and also heart disease as well as slowing the progression of Alzheimer's and Parkinson's disease. For women, one five-ounce glass a day is good, but the health benefits are forfeited if you drink more. ☺

144 Recite a Favorite Prayer While Walking Around the Block

Do you turn to God when you are dealing with a crisis? If you do, you are like many others who take comfort in knowing that they are not alone in dealing with their troubles or solving their problems. Allocate part of a daily exercise for a devotional walk around the block. Whatever your spiritual belief, during that period, eyes and heart wide open, invite the Divine to be with you as you pray a favorite prayer or psalm. Praying can be done as holy conversation and sacred song as well. The point is to realize that you are not alone in your crisis and to seek comfort, protection, peace, and joy in your spiritual relationship with the Divine. ☺

145 Notice One Thing Each Day That Gives You Pleasure

In spite of the negative circumstances you may be dealing with, find little moments throughout the day to notice the things that, under ordinary circumstances, give you pleasure. For example, take time to appreciate the view of the neighbor's yellow roses that have just burst into bloom, the taste of a perfectly ripe sweet apple, the sound of classical music as the CD plays on your laptop, the painting you bought in Paris that hangs in your office, the feel of your favorite loafers, or the warmth and smallness of your child's hand in yours. Savor the gifts of sight, sense, taste, touch, and smell. They are working even as you deal with crisis. Take comfort in simply noticing the blessings in the small things and short moments throughout the day. ☺

Find Moments of Happiness in Crisis

146 Journal the Details of the Crisis Outcome You Desire and Why

What do you want as an outcome to the crisis? Why do you want that particular outcome and not another? Write the answers to those two questions in your journal. Then use what you have written as points of departure for delving deeper. It is often difficult to get clarity when your brain is befuddled by an unexpected turn of events or bad news. Journaling is one way to fully consider all your options. Get all the ideas out of your brain and on paper so that you can think about them and look at them. Reorganize ideas. See what's missing. What you don't know. What you can investigate or learn more about. Use your journal as a powerful tool to help facilitate making the hard decisions and getting the best moral, ethical, and spiritual outcome. ☺

147 Write a Paragraph about Your Loss, and Then Rewrite It as a Gain

When you suffer loss, take time to have a cup of tea and write about your loss. Then, consider what you might gain as you are compelled to move forward. For example, after a spouse dies, gone too are the shared dreams, income, and perhaps even the house. Loss pushes you outside of your comfort zone where new opportunities for your new life await. What if you always wanted a small farm in Connecticut? What's stopping you? What if you never finished college? What's holding you back now? You like marriage and want a new partner at some point. What if you could screen her to fit your desired profile? What if she is perfect for the next chapter of your life? Dare to dream a bold new future. ☺

CHAPTER 9

Be Happy on the Road

148 Take Along Your Favorite Travel Pillow

Hedge your bet that you'll get a good night's sleep when traveling. Remember to take along your favorite little travel pillow. It stuffs easily into a carry-on bag and can serve as a terrific insurance policy against sleepless nights. Traveling can sap your energy by various means, including jet lag. One of the best ways to beat jet lag is to get plenty of rest. When traveling on a business trip or family vacation, the choice of pillow in your hotel room or in the sleeping room of a ship or ferry or airplane may not be yours, but you can always pull out your favorite travel pillow and know that blissful sleep is only moments away. ☺

149 Find Opportunities Arising from Travel Delays

When your train doesn't arrive on time or your flight is delayed, see opportunities. Get out your laptop or notepad and make a list of positive things that could come about because of the delay. Think of the delay as a blessing that gives you extra time to use in myriad ways. You could:

- Make some phone calls
- Catch up on paperwork
- Study a map
- Network with others
- Brainstorm some new adventures
- Write some postcards, e-mails, or even outline a book ☺

150 Give Flowers to Your Foreign Host or Hostess

If you've stayed in an apartment in Provence, a bed and breakfast in Belfast, or a small lodge in Kathmandu, show your appreciation to your host with a bouquet. If you want to make it really special, ask your host what his favorite colors and flowers are. Presenting a surprise bouquet to him upon your departure is bound to say more than your expressions of gratitude. The language of flowers speaks directly to the heart. Expect smiles. ☺

 ## 151 Taste at Least One New Food or Beverage

You are traveling. Reset your gastronomic preferences. Get into the swing of things during your visit to a new place. Sample some of the local cuisine. Find a little restaurant that offers tapas or

appetizers on a sampler plate and try all of them. In the United Kingdom, go for some pub grub and a pint. Ask the locals about tasty regional specialties in Greece, Turkey, and Morocco. In Belgium or Switzerland, tantalize your taste buds with some fine chocolate. Or for a really adventurous taste experience, try some haggis in Scotland and the pickled pig's feet of northern Spain. Experiment and have some fun doing it. ☺

152 Buy a Book about Local Customs

In Nepal, lying with the soles of your bare feet pointed at your host's head or images of the Divine is insulting. Likewise, if you are trekking or camping with Sherpa guides, don't cook meat over an open fire as they considered burning meat offensive to the gods. Before you take that next trip, buy a book that provides information about local customs so you won't risk facing

Be Happy on the Road

a judge in a foreign land. When in doubt, always follow your in-country host's lead in terms of cultural behavior and local customs and you'll be fine. ☺

153 Loan a Fellow Traveler Something She Needs

Show a generosity of spirit to a weary or stressed-out fellow traveler by loaning her something she needs for her trip but has forgotten, such as sunscreen, an extra tube of toothpaste, an unopened package of earplugs, a sealed teabag, or a travel-size sewing kit. Your act of kindness could cement a joyful new friendship. ☺

154 Give an Elderly Person Your Seat on Public Transportation

Be a good person. Get up, and with a smile, offer your seat on the bus, train, or subway to an elderly individual. It's the right thing to do. Think of the good karma you are generating. Old people are not as stable on their feet as they were in their youth. Vacate your seat and allow them the safety of sitting instead of holding onto a rail or strap over their heads, something you might easily do. You'll feel good just knowing that you showed an act of kindness to another. And you are a better person for having done it. ☺

155 Introduce Yourself to Someone Waiting in Line

Strike up a conversation with someone you don't know but who looks interesting, is attractive, seems lost, or appears confused. Help out if the latter is the case. Perhaps you are traveling somewhere in the world where you've been before and know how the trains operate or which is the best way to get to the center plaza of the village or town. Others around may join in the conversation and, thus, you meet people in a group who may also be going your way. You never know until you open your mouth and engage others in conversation. Making friends on the road in new towns, villages, and cities can enrich your traveling experience. ☺

 **156** Help a Traveler in Distress

If you notice a distressed visitor trying to figure out a map or the direction to his destination in an area familiar to you, offer to help him. Point him in the right direction. When you give directions, write them on a card or carefully explain the distances, turns, and notable landmarks. Communicate as clearly as possible. Nothing is more frustrating and, in some cases, frightening than to be lost in a new city or unfamiliar place. Be the person you would like to meet if that happened to you. Who knows? Your distressed traveler may be inspired by your kindness to one day help another in the same way. Remember that old adage about how one good turn deserves another. It's one way happiness can be spread. ☺

 157 Buy a Bus Ticket for a Quick Local Tour

If you only have a couple of days in a town, for example, New York, Chicago, or Savannah, take a bus tour and let a trained professional driver or guide show you the sights and tell you about what you are seeing. The overview can help you decide which sites you would like to see more of as well as those areas to avoid. Additionally, a bus tour can provide:

Be Happy on the Road

- Easy access to city sites and tourist attractions
- Flexibility in schedules
- Audio in a variety of languages
- Efficiency and cost-effectiveness ☺

158 Accept an Invitation to Dine in a Local Family Home

Do you love Russian vodka and caviar blinis? The next time you are sailing down the Volga on a cruise ship and a nice Russian family invites you to dinner, don't hesitate to say da, or yes. You'll have a memorable experience dining with that family on foods that you may not have tasted elsewhere in your travels. Anytime you are visiting a region or country that is new to you, don't miss out on the opportunity to see how families live, eat, and share fellowship with their friends. After all, breaking bread together is an ancient ritual practiced in cultures throughout the world. ☺

159 Pack Less

Lugging a big suitcase around wherever you go can cause more than one kind of headache. Many airlines now charge you a fee to handle your checked bag, so traveling light makes more sense now than ever. One tip is to purchase basic travel clothing that is lightweight and washable in neutral colors such as basic black and tan that can be dressed up easily for dressier occasions on your trip. Often, that type of travel clothing is virtually wrinkle-free and takes up little space in a bag. Pack less, travel light, and avoid the headaches. ☺

Use a Money Belt

Use a money belt when you travel on vacation. You want to safeguard your money, and slipping it into a lightweight money belt that fits around your waist or inside your trousers is a far better option than carrying it in a purse or backpack, especially if either of those have a long shoulder strap. Thieves can come up beside you, cut the strap, and be gone before you realize what has just happened. Pickpockets can clean your cash, credit cards, passport, and identification out of your pocket just as easily. It's a crime as old as currency itself. You want to be happy when traveling, not sitting at some police station seeking help in recovering your stolen property. ☺

161 Carry a Bag for Someone Who Needs Help

Come to the aid of someone struggling with her luggage. Maybe she's trying to get it on the tram to the airport and you are going her way. Or, perhaps your traveling buddy is headed back from the local flea market with his rented bike overloaded with bags. You could take one and lighten his load. Or, you see a little old Greek lady crossing the street after buying her groceries and the handle on one of her bags breaks. Don't wait for someone else to rush over and help her. You do it. And put a smile on your face. Little old Greek ladies deserve as much. ☺

162 Take a Cheap Road Trip with Your Kids

Think of someplace you could take the kids during a weekend, a school-break holiday, or summer vacation where the destination is perhaps less important that the journey. Make getting there as fun as possible for your tots, tweens, or teens. Pack books, games, CDs, art and craft supplies, and a big cooler that you fill with bottles of water, sandwiches, and snacks for the journey. Don't forget pillows and blankets for those who need naps. The point is to make it an interactive experience that your family will always remember with smiles and laughter. ☺

163 Explore an Interesting Path or Side Street

Sometimes, the most memorable places you'll find while on vacation are the little discoveries you made off an alley, down an interesting side street, or along a path that lead to a river's edge, a shady courtyard, or a butterfly garden. Be adventurous when traveling. Explore the neighborhood where your accommodations are located. Drive to a nearby town or village and sample their foods and wines. Discover a deserted hill town. Or make your way to what appears to be a palace of a bygone era. Take off with your walking stick into the hill country. Discover places beyond the familiar path that will make your trip unique and special. ☺

164 Invite a Fellow Traveler for Dinner at a Local Café

If you bump into someone you recognize from the airport, on a local bus trip, or from the lobby of your hotel, invite her to dine with you. Traveling solo can be lonely at times and the camaraderie of new friends can lift your spirits. Your fellow traveler may be craving company as much as you are. Some experiences are best enjoyed with another person. If you go to Ireland, for example, with an urge to bike around the southern part of the Emerald Isle to see the Ring of Kerry and the Cliffs of Mohr, having a fellow traveler along might provide the impetus to just go for it. You buy or rent some bikes in Dublin and head off into the biking trip of a lifetime, then share stories about it in the local pub when it's over. Now how fun could that be? ☺

165 Exchange E-mail Addresses with a Foreign Family

Nothing brings back memories of your trip like receiving mail from friends you made while on vacation. But if they don't know how to contact you once you've left them, you won't be getting those photos they took of you during your visit, the piece of art they promised to send, their postcards, or letters. So, don't forget to exchange your e-mail address with families and friends you met while traveling. You'll enjoy memories of that trip all over again when they contact you. And, if you are lucky, you'll be invited back next year. ☺

166 Pack Your Favorite Herb Tea, Medicines, and Personal Products

If it's pouring rain in Paris and you forget your umbrella and end up with a nasty cold on the way back from walking to the Notre Dame, most likely, you aren't a happy traveler. Likewise when those monthly cramps begin the moment you set foot on the beach in Jamaica in your bikini. Anticipate times during your upcoming trip when you might not feel well. Before you go, pack those personal items such as tea, medicines, and other products that will comfort you and make you feel better when you are away from home. ☺

167 Generously Tip Hotel, Motel, and B&B Housekeepers

No one enjoys picking up dirty, wet towels and cleaning sinks and showers of soap scum, whiskers, and hair. When you are working out the budget for your trip, try to include tips for the household workers who keep your home away from home clean, sanitary, and fresh. Housekeepers and motel workers make very little money, yet their work, in addition to being tedious and dirty, is often thankless. Your generous tip will help them better provide for their families and tells them that you have appreciated their work. And you can feel happier knowing that your act may change the ugly American perception by some foreigners to a view that Americans are friendly, caring, and generous. ☺

CHAPTER 10

Find Happiness Pursuing Your Dreams

168 Devise Six Specific Points for Your Ideal Future

On a piece of notepaper, jot down six specific things about the future life you desire. If it makes the task any easier, first think of several areas of your life, for example: family, friends, finances, health, career, and spirituality/religion. There are certainly many other areas you could list, but choose six and then write out something specific about that area of your life that you would like to manifest. For example, you might write, "I will have an income over $75,000 next year" or "I will move into a house twice the size of the one I'm in now." When you are clear about what you want, you are more likely to get it. ☺

169 Three Times a Day Visualize Achieving a Personal Goal

What's your primary personal goal? Is it to lose weight, spend less, or earn more money? Whatever it is, write out an affirmation for achieving it. For example: From now on at mealtimes I will eat one-third less than my usual serving of food, and I will walk for a half-hour each weekday. Try to keep your affirmation succinct and to the point. That way, it will be easy to recall, and repeat it at least three times during the day. The more specific your affirmation, the more effective it will be in helping you attain your goal. ☺

170 Devise Spinoffs from Your Dream

Consider how you might do what one television infomercial guy did, that is, spinning your dream along different avenues. The television guy speaks passionately about his love of real estate wheeling and dealing, updating houses that he buys cheap through foreclosures, bank-owned real estate auctions, or tax sales. He flipped those houses into a million-dollar income, but he didn't stop there. He spun his dream into books, seminars, conferences, a television show, and other areas that cross-sold his real estate ideas. Your interest might not be in real estate or lend itself to exactly those types of spinoffs, but think of how you, too, could develop spinoffs from your dream. ☺

 171 Establish Attainable Goals

When you have decided that success is possible and have worked on your inner game (that is, being able to think of yourself as successful), then it's time to establish some modest, attainable goals. Reaching for too much too soon might render disappointment if you aren't immediately successful. Starting out with some attainable goals will increase your confidence and inspire you to even greater accomplishments. ☺

172 Ask Someone You Admire to Share Her Success Story

Whenever you meet someone who has successfully followed and manifested her dream, ask her to tell you about her personal journey. Unless you already know everything there is to know about becoming successful and turning your dreams into reality, you can learn a great deal from others. Perhaps there are pitfalls and minefields you can avoid that someone else has already gone through. Be open to suggestions, insights, caveats, and the counsel of successful people. Most likely, they were once in your shoes, embarking upon a path toward their dreams and hoping to achieve success ☺

173 Ask Five Friends to Help You

Think of your dream as a team project. Ask yourself how five friends could help you reach your goal. Write down a master list of everything that must be done. Now make those calls to your buddies. For example, perhaps you love to cook and already teach small classes in your kitchen. You'd like to take your cooking enterprise into a bigger venue. You could write a cookbook and have your friends become testers (preparing and cooking your recipes so see if the dishes come out correctly each time). Or, you could assign each friend a specific task to help you make a video for a cooking show that might air on your local cable network. Enlisting the help of friends means they are invested in helping you succeed. So, get your team together and go for your dream. ☺

174 Schedule Thirty Minutes Each Day to Work on Your Dream

Isn't your dream worth thirty minutes of your time? If you think you can't squeeze thirty minutes out of a twenty-four-hour day, think again. How long do you spend in the shower or shaving or putting on makeup? How long is the prep for dinner? Use snatches of time here and there if you can't find a block of thirty minutes. The point is to work on lifting that dream out of the wish state and pulling it into manifestation in your life as soon as you can. Yoke your dream to your will, intent, and action and then give yourself a pat on the back for drawing your dream into physical reality. ☺

175 Buy a Blank Journal and Record Your Daily Progress

Blank journals are great for keeping track of the progress you make toward achieving your dream. You can find blank journals in bookstores, drug stores, and some supermarkets and department stores. Perhaps you've always dreamed of owning your own salon. Assuming you already have your cosmetology license and, perhaps, a station at a local salon, begin by figuring out all of your options, including striking out on your own or partnering with a friend, relative, or an associate. Is there a local salon for sale? Is there retail space at a good price in a great location? Do you already have a clientele who will follow you to your new location? Where will you get the money for your startup operations? Brainstorm until you know everything about actualizing your dream. Write your ideas in the journal. Then, make your dream happen. ☺

176 Incubate Your Dream and Let It Take Flight

This exercise might not seem too specific, but in fact it is. Incubate means allowing something time to reach its fullness. Letting your dream take flight is letting go of the restrictions you might place upon yourself and your dream. Instead, think about it until it reaches its fullness then let it go. Follow it. Writer Anaïs Nin once observed that a dream was always ahead of her and she chased it, but when she caught up and lived in unison with it for a moment, that moment was nothing short of a miracle. Dreams open your mind to beautiful and exciting possibilities. Give your dream free reign. You may even discover happiness and unfathomable success. ☺

Find Happiness Pursuing Your Dreams

177 Give Your Dream Some Rocket Power

A dream needs a powerful push to move into manifestation. You give it that power by making your dream as clear as possible in your mind, turning it into a specific goal or goals, putting the goals into a time line, and knowing what the culmination of that dream looks like. For example, you wish you could leave your indoor office job and find some kind of work in nature, possibly landscaping, or overseeing the care and security of a park. Get more specific. Working at a wildlife rescue center is quite different than that of caring for the horses at an equine therapy center. Clipping spent flowers from rose bushes at a community garden is different from enforcing the rules governing the use of a local park. St. Augustine, in the fifth century, offered the following sage advice, "Pray as if everything depended upon God and act as if everything depended upon you." Ignatius Loyola changed the word "act" to "work." The point is that belief, actions, and work are all necessary to push forth a dream from the idea realm into manifestation. ☺

178 Create a Manifestation Board for Your Dream

A sheet of poster paper or foam board will serve as a board on which you can paste images, inspirational words, goals, and dates for accomplishing goals as well as ideas of new directions to take your dream. Maybe you want to find a way to help your children's school establish a theatrical group or an arts program. Perhaps you are an artist and can guide children in making masks, costumes, stage sets, and the like. Cut pictures of those images from magazines and put them on your board. Do you know other parents or artist friends and teachers who could help you launch such a program? Write their names on your board. Check them off as you call and make your pitch. You'll soon learn that a dream doesn't have to be a solo dream; it can come about through a team working together on a commonly held vision. ☺

proper price point for your product. Determining the optimum business location or having a great website will also be important. You want to start a business that succeeds. Knowing what is vital to that success will help you get those things before you launch your company. ☺

 179 Post on Your Mirror Five Factors Vital to Your Success

Think of five factors that are absolutely vital to the success of your dream. Write them on sticky paper or note cards and place them where you can see and think about them. For example, having a dream of owning your own business might mean knowing everything you can possibly know about your product or service and the demographic of your ideal customer, having a business plan, finding enough capital, and establishing the

180 Write Your Desired Result and Plot a Course Backward

A terrific exercise for seeing if you have figured out all the potential obstacles in your way to having your dream come true is to figure out exactly what the end result is and then plotting events backward to the beginning and the first step. Perhaps your dream is to win the lottery. Start with winning it and work backward listing the events. You play every day, spending a dollar on the Quick Pick. Even before the day you place your first bet, you choose your favorite numbers. Every day for two weeks, you walk to the convenience store in your neighborhood to play. You play at 7:00 P.M. Then, on the fourteenth day, your numbers come up. ☺

181 Ask Six Friends to Support Your Dream Endeavor

You have dreams and so do your friends. Choose six friends and ask them if they would be interested in having a team to support them in pursuing their dreams. Then call a meeting of everyone and have a discussion of how each of you could best serve each other as all of you deliberately go after your dreams. Will you call each other every day to talk about progress and concrete issues? Will you meet on Saturdays for bagels and coffee to discuss overcoming any obstacles that some or all of you have faced during the week? Knowing you have a close-knit network of individuals committed to help you realize your heart's desire can help you stay motivated and on course. ☺

182 Put a Talisman on Your Desk to Remind You of Your Dream

Maybe you have always wanted to have lots of money, not for merely having it but rather for the purpose of being able to exchange it for other things important to you. Consider purchasing a talisman or charm for wealth, abundance, and success. A talisman is simply an object intended to ward off evil and bring good luck. If you choose to make your money talisman, do so during the waxing phase of the moon. When you are ready to charge it, hold the talisman in your right hand (which you place facing up in your left hand) and charge it with your prayers, deep breathing, visualization of its purpose, and infusion of your life force energy. When not in use, keep your talisman in a silk bag near where you work or on your desk to remind you to pursue your dream. ☺

183 List Specific Ways You'll Celebrate Achieving Your Dream

You finally made your dream a reality. How will you celebrate to mark the occasion? Will you buy yourself that expensive piece of jewelry you've been wanting? Or, will you escape to Monte Carlo for a long weekend? Perhaps you want to do something physical like climb a mountain. Make celebration an important activity in the process of realizing your dream. You are marking a milestone and getting ready for the next part of your great adventure because a dream has a way of spawning others. ☺

184 Share Your Dreams with Your Children

Draw your children into your conversation about your dream. Share with them your ideas about how to you plan to achieve your dream. Seek their input as well. Their ideas may strike you as silly, crazy, imaginative, inventive, or solid—you'll never know unless you chat with them about it. When you involve your children in creative brainstorming, you are teaching them how to formulate and work on their own dreams. Children's minds are ever-evolving. As they grow, their minds develop. They begin to differentiate between rational thinking and emotional thinking. By including them in your dream sharing, you help them develop healthy minds than can adapt, solve problems, and evolve further. ☺

185 Support Your Spouse's Dream

You love your spouse and want his dreams to be fulfilled, too. Think of several ways you could help him realize his deepest desires. Perhaps he always wanted to see a baseball game in all the National League stadiums west of the Rockies. You could suggest that next year he take a summer vacation with his best buddy and go on a baseball junket, visiting his favorite stadiums to see a game. Help him plan his junket with maps, time lines, and cost estimates. Provided your relationship is firmly rooted in trust, vacations apart can be fun and healthy. Spell out other ways you can envision supporting his dreams. Then, of course, you can talk about yours. ☺

CHAPTER 11

Promote Happiness at Your Workplace

186 Buy a Cup of Coffee for Your Boss

If your boss never notices you, buy her a cup of java and that might change. Or just do it as a spontaneous act of thoughtfulness. Consider what it might be like to do her job. It is unlikely that your boss was hired because of some kind of likeability quotient but rather because she had the right credentials, experience, and know-how to do whatever the job entailed. If you find your work at times challenging and stressful, imagine what your boss feels. Wouldn't you just love to have someone buy you a cup of coffee when you feel challenged, frustrated, glum, unfocused, behind schedule, or stressed? So buy that cup of coffee for your boss and put a smile on both of your faces. ☺

187 Admit to Your Superiors That You Screwed Up

It's often difficult to admit to your superiors that you made a mistake. However, doing so demonstrates your sense of responsibility and willingness to shoulder blame. Taking responsibility for a screwup by you or your team shows your managers and boss that you are a person with values and moral principles. Although a mistake has been made, you'll be better off admitting it and moving forward than deceiving, lying, or covering up the error, all of which can have disastrous consequences for you later when the truth is finally found out. ☺

188 Greet a Cranky Coworker with a Plate of Warm Cookies

Bake some cookies in the office microwave or bring them from home. If someone in your office often scowls, chronically complains, or flies into a hissy fit with little or no provocation, offer him a plate of warm chocolate chip or peanut butter cookies. Even if they are refused, you can be assured that you at least tried to bring a little pleasure into that person's life. The gesture may work or it may not. Some people get so used to being unhappy and feeling like the whole world is against them that they are outside their comfort zone when someone does something unexpected and nice for them. The truth is that they are more likely than not hungry for friendship and attention. ☺

189 Show Up on Time and Prepared for Meetings

Many working professionals feel that although meetings can be big time wasters, they are often necessary for the smooth functioning of their departments, businesses, or corporations. Leaders can use meetings to gather information and input from others, address a hot topic of concern to all gathered, or celebrate a milestone or a worker's accomplishments. A leader can also use a meeting to challenge, motivate, and inspire others. Whether you are the leader or an individual attending the meeting, take the time to prepare (if you are expected to provide input, ideas, or data) and always show up on time. Being on time and prepared demonstrates a high level of integrity and commitment. Be proud of yourself for making the effort. ☺

190 Speak the Truth for a Whole Day—No Fibs Allowed

Can you go through an entire day telling the truth and only the truth? Telling the truth, like thinking positive thoughts, is a skill that requires lots of practice. Many people tell little white lies, half-truths, or useful falsehoods to evade blame, deceive, deny reality, or to feel better about themselves. A little white lie, in some instances, might be motivated by a desire to prevent someone from being hurt. For example, you know that a coworker is about to be fired. When she asks you if you've heard anything about her possible termination, you tell her no. It takes more effort to think about how to answer her truthfully and still not hurt her feelings than to just lie. But if you live and work from a place of truth, others will trust your word and appreciate the honesty. In the long term, truth may be the most powerful tool you have in your career toolbox. ☺

191 Single Out One Coworker Each Week for Praise

When you see a coworker's extraordinary effort to get a project completed or to do a particular task well, offer some heartfelt praise. A word or two of encouragement can mean a lot to that person. Plus, people tend to be more productive when they know that their efforts are appreciated. If you are a manager or leader and don't feel you are getting the best effort from your workers, think about what you can do to raise the morale and set the tone for a friendlier, supportive work environment. Make it a priority to appropriately praise and reward dedication and effort on the job. ☺

192 Write a Thank-You Note to Someone on Your Team

A member of your team helped you meet a deadline, stood in for you in a meeting, or even took on a part of your workload, so take the time to write her a thank-you note. Keep the tone professional and adhere to good writing standards, avoiding slang and words whose meaning might be misconstrued. Don't send your thank-you note by e-mail. Although e-mails are appropriate for various types of office communication, a hand-written thank-you note is a personal expression of appreciation. By contrast, consider how a hastily written message of thanks, sent by e-mail, might be received. When you let workers know that you view them and their contributions as important to the team's success and take the time to write a thoughtful note, most likely you'll be rewarded with loyalty and assistance the next time you need it. ☺

193 Clear Your Desktop at the End of Every Work Day

Time management experts say that a clean desk is important for several reasons. You work more efficiently when you know where documents and tools are at all times rather than having to search through piles of disorganized material on your desktop. A clean desk signals to clients and others that most likely you are an organized person with efficient and effective work habits, thus inspiring confidence. Don't wait to clean that desk off. Get yourself some garbage bags, several filing boxes, manila and hanging folders, labels, and an organizer for your to-do lists, addresses, and other data, and a calendar. Join the ranks of happily organized workers. ☺

Promote Happiness at Your Workplace

194 Keep Competition Among Coworkers Friendly

A load is lighter when several people help carry it. Teamwork may seem incompatible with competition, but when competition is friendly it can spur everyone on toward a mutual goal and make the load lighter for everyone. Helen Keller once noted that we can do little alone but together we can accomplish much. The key is to find ways to spur everyone to compete to the fullest, doing their best, and always insisting that winners and losers stick to the rules of good sportsmanship. Celebrate the effort of each individual worker attempting to exceed his best level of accomplishment rather than feeling joyful because of the outcome (someone wins or loses). ☺

195 Itemize for Your Boss the Tasks You Love Doing

Do you love pulling together data for your company's due diligence binders, working on payroll and reconciling the bank statements, writing press releases, researching, or working on the company website? Let your boss know what tasks you especially like. It's possible that just by letting your preferences be known that you will get more of that kind of work. And if you really like doing those tasks, you are probably happier and enthusiastic while at work. Those feelings can spread around the office. Just imagine if everyone is doing what they most like to do. Start an "I love my job" campaign. Get everyone on board. ☺

196 Think of Three Tasks Someone Else Could Do and Delegate Them

When a job or project is too big for one brain and one set of hands, it's a good idea to delegate. If you're not a manager and this isn't your job, speak to your manager about it. The dictionary says that the word "delegate" means to entrust or hand over to another. When your workload is lighter, you can focus more intently on every aspect of your job and most likely do it better than when you were overloaded. Think of three tasks that you could easily hand off to someone else equally qualified to do them, and let him go to work. Allowing that person to honor you by doing the job to the best of his ability means that you won't micromanage him. Trust him and give him time to do his best work. Then, everyone will benefit. ☺

197 Schedule Moments of Relaxation During the Workday

How do you feel at the end of a typical workday? If you often feel drained, totally stressed out, and in a bad mood, try to find a few moments throughout the day to de-stress and relax. Some people find that a quick cat nap or a half-hour power nap over lunch can push away fatigue and re-energize them. Others swear that a brisk walk when they can practice mindfulness and deep breathing is equally beneficial for banishing stress and helping them to refocus. Try getting in a little workout going up and down some stairs. Step outside for fresh air and sunlight. Sit somewhere for five minutes and close your eyes. Just breathe in an out, mindful of the breaths. Feel relaxed. ☺

Promote Happiness at Your Workplace

198 Volunteer to Set Up a Company Library

If you can't find the most recent due diligence binder, the latest industry trade magazine with a profile of your boss, or timely reference books that you need to complete a project, consider volunteering to establish a library for your business. Not only will it benefit others in your company, but it could be a career booster for you, especially if you not only brainstormed the idea but also got it approved and have sacrificed some personal time to spearhead the project. Your initiative and foresight most likely will set you apart as a visionary with a can-do attitude, the type of individual that many companies like to recruit and retain. ☺

199 Make Note of the Birthdays of Your Coworkers

Purchase a pocketbook-size calendar and keep track of coworkers' birthdays. It means a lot to people when others remember their birthdays. You don't have to have an elaborate celebration; a card that everyone signs can be just as meaningful. The point isn't really that you got them a card or a cake but rather that you and your coworkers took the time to keep track and then to pay homage. Spreading around a little celebratory happiness on birthdays does wonders for office morale. Try it and see for yourself. ☺

200 Ask Your Boss for a Special Assignment

If you hope to land a special project, consider asking your boss to assign you. Be clear in your communication. Tell your boss why you believe you are precisely the right person for that job. Go beyond your qualifications and also mention why you would feel more passionate about it than other equally qualified individuals. If your boss passes over you and gives that special assignment that you covet to someone else, be a good sport. Congratulate the other person and offer your help in the event he or she might need or welcome it. That way, you both can enjoy the project. ☺

more harmonious, happier, and more productive work life. For example, maybe you are the type to hit the ground running every morning. Instead of starting to work on your many projects the minute you arrive at the office, consider starting your day differently. Listen to some music. Spend a few minutes of deep breathing while you concentrate on feelings of being happy, relaxed but focused, prepared, and centered. Shaking up your routine to feel happier can be a good thing. ☺

 ## Do One New Thing Each Week to Create a Happier Work Life

If you have to play mind games to psych yourself up to go to work, it might be time to think about changing jobs. Conversely, if you like your work but wished you could enjoy it more, think of one new activity or ritual that you could do each week to create a

202 ## Set Computer Reminders

Can't remember coworkers' birthdays, the date of your company office party, the timing of the arrival of a team from out-of-state, or when you last ran a full security scan on your office computer? Many people don't take full advantage of the built-in features of their computers or those that their company provides. Take advantage of the sophisticated programming already in your computer or software to manage appointments and contacts using the personal information manager (PIM feature). Most computers also offer a powerful and easy-to-use filing system so that you can even work in a paperless environment. If you seek a higher profile in your workplace, there's an easy way to accomplish that. When you know where things are all the time or how to retrieve them in a mouse click or two, you might just get bragging rights to being the new "go-to person" for the entire office. ☺

203 List Three Reasons Why You Should Be Promoted

You know you are good. But can you articulate succinctly and persuasively why you should be promoted? If not, try writing down three good reasons why you deserve a promotion. After you have requested a private meeting with your boss, let her know you understand she's a busy person. Instead of making small talk, get directly to the point. Let her know that you enjoy working for the company. Focus on the quality and quantity of your work. Tell your boss the three reasons why you should be promoted to a new job. Know what the new job will entail and be able to share details of what qualifies you to perform the tasks expected in the new job. Explain you'll happily take new training and are eager to accept new responsibilities. ☺

204 Choose a Date to Ask for a Promotion

You know why you should be promoted, but the timing for seeking the promotion could possibly impact the outcome. Is there a major project that needs to be pushed through first? Does someone have to leave before you can move up and into his or her position? Decide when you think the time would best serve you, your boss, and your company for you to seek a promotion. Circle a date on your desk calendar and look at it every day. Know that date is coming and you need to prepare. Get ready. ☺

205 Resolve to Improve Workplace Ethics

If your company follows a policy of putting profits ahead of ethical practices, possibly even at the expense of exploiting workers or customers, why not seek a review of current company policies with your boss or supervisor. Such a companywide review of ethical practices and standards of behavior would likely permit discussion of questionable policies. You might be able (even encouraged) to challenge practices that you think are unfair, exploitive, or unethical. For each questionable practice or policy, find and offer an ethical alternative. When acceptable ethical practices and moral conduct are clearly stated and followed, workplace morale can often improve as well. ☺

206 Find One Person to Be Your Workplace Ally or Confidante

If there is someone in the company or on your job site that you trust and who shares your level of integrity and ethics, aligning with him could benefit your professional goals, especially if that person is a supervisor or further along the career ladder than you are . Having someone as a workplace ally means you don't have to feel alone as you navigate through office politics, solve problems, or deal with difficult coworkers. A workplace ally can serve as your sounding board for new ideas, cheer you on when your day is filled with special challenges, and give you a pep talk to lift your heart and hopes when you need it. Cherish him and nurture that friendship.   ☺

CHAPTER 12

Exercise Your Way to a Happier You

207 Ask a Friend to Join You in a Fitness Program

Once you have resolved to live a healthier lifestyle, learn about good nutrition, introduce lots of fresh vegetables and fruits into your and your family's meals, and invite a friend to be your exercise buddy. Walk during your lunch hour. Ride bikes or roller blade around a local park. Take a swim aerobics class. Do yoga together. The point is to make exercise fun, a social event as much as a workout. When you are laughing and conversing, the time goes by much more quickly. Socializing stimulates the mind just as exercise increases blood flow. Both nourish you and should be part of a healthy lifestyle. ☺

208 Invite a Friend to Help You Prepare Healthier Foods

What you eat influences how you feel, and feeling happy is all about eating healthy. Learn to choose healthy fruits and vegetables by visiting your local organic grocery and farmer's market and then enlist a friend to help you discover interesting ways to prepare heart healthy entrées using whole grains, nuts, eggs, legumes, fish, and chicken. Try also to purchase beef, pork, and veal that are certified organic, range fed, and free of additives. Use extra-virgin olive oil if possible for recipes calling for oil. And as a general rule, stay away from packaged products in favor of fresh. Split the cost of a cookbook for healthy meals with your friend, and get ready to cook a little something sure to delight your senses. ☺

209 Sign Up for Tennis Lessons

Playing a game of tennis is a great way to get a workout. Warm up your muscles first and take care to use proper hitting and serving techniques to prevent injuries. Tennis pros say that a couple of days each week on the court should be enough for a good workout. Days off the court allow your overused muscles to rest and recover. Almost anyone, from eight- to ten-year-old children to seniors in their seventies or eighties, can play tennis. Lean how to play now and you can enjoy it for a lifetime. Plus, tennis is one of those games where you need another player. If you are playing doubles, you'll need three other players; it's a good way to meet new people, get a workout, and feel great. ☺

210 Buy a New Swimsuit and Go Play in the Water

Swimsuit shopping can lift your spirits, especially if you've gotten in shape prior to the summer swimsuit season. So go buy a suit and join family or friends for some water play. Skin cancer is a serious risk, so be sure to use adequate sunscreen to protect against the sun's harmful rays. Wear a hat with a wide brim to shade your face and neck. Also, avoid the hottest times of the day when the sun is directly overhead. Opt for playing in the water during the early morning and late afternoon hours when you can swim, snorkel, water-ski, deep-sea dive, surf, or row around in your kayak or canoe. Also, drink plenty of water to replenish what you lose through perspiration from all that exercise. Now go and have a blast. ☺

211 Exchange a House with a Foreign Family

If you've dreamed of exploring exotic European locales, sampling the cuisine, and shopping in local markets and antique stores, consider swapping your house with a foreign family. You will stay in the home of an Italian, French, Spanish, or German family and that family gets to come to America and stay in your house. Whether you want to swap for a week or a month or longer, home exchange organizations and property management companies that specialize in vacation house exchanges can answer your questions and facilitate the house swapping. Ask if the homeowner would allow you to ride the family bicycles, row the family boat, or ride the horses. The point is to not just laze around in the swapped house, but enjoy your new surroundings to the fullest and keep your exercise going. ☺

212 Play Twister or Musical Chairs at Your Next Party

The next time your family gets together for some good old-fashioned fun, suggest a game of Twister or musical chairs. Spread out the Twister mat and review the game rules. Spin the needle and prepare to twist yourself into knots. Or, try a few rounds of musical chairs. Before starting the music, make sure there is one less chair than the number of players. For every cycle of music, remove another chair so that there's always one less chair than there are players. These activities may not burn a lot of calories but do provide a little exercise with the emphasis on fun. ☺

213 Take a Kickboxing Class

Release some of that aggression in a kickboxing class where you'll learn to combine martial arts kicks with boxing punches for a great workout. There are many different styles of kickboxing and variants to choose from, for example, Brazilian Jiu-Jitsu, Muay Thai, Burmese kickboxing, American kickboxing, Indian adithada, and French savate, to name a few. Many of the kickboxing forms and styles have evolved into national and international competitions. As a kickboxer, you typically "fight" in rounds of varying duration (these are usually agreed upon prior to the fight). You get a great cardio workout regardless of the form of kickboxing you choose, and when you study it with a spouse or a friend you can practice (and get in shape) together. ☺

pays a big dividend, then consider taking a class on how to lay tile or renovate/remodel your bathroom. Laying tile involves many activities, including but not limited to carrying, cutting, and applying tile with special tile glue. But before you lay any tile, you may have to first remove old tile and/or cabinets, tub, toilet, and shower. You will be bending, lifting, walking, reaching, and stretching during the process. You most certainly will be tired at the end of the day. But as you stretch out the soreness in your muscles, imagine how happy you'll be to have a brand new bathroom and to know it will add dollars to the value of your home. ☺

214 Tile Your Bathroom

If your idea of exercise involves moving your body and doing something else productive that

215 Go Horseback Riding

Just imagine bundling up in a sweater and scarf on a chilly spring or fall morning and riding horseback along a beach past crashing waves or through a leafy forest glade, replete with dew-laden spider webs and small critters scurrying out of your path. The world looks and feels different from the back of a horse. Horseback riding seems to heighten your senses of sight, smell, and touch. Riding at full gallop requires you to use those thigh muscles, and your feet and hands to stay in the saddle. Mounting and dismounting also can provide a little workout. But the joy you feel seated atop a horse and observing the world awakening is a bonus for exercising by riding horseback. ☺

216 Design and Plant an Herb Garden

Gardening gives you the opportunity to work out in the fresh air. And nothing beats fresh-picked herbs when you want to intensify the taste of salsas, sauces, and savory dishes. Using a spade to turn over dirt and dig in fertilizers and soil amendments can give you a workout. The number of calories burned while gardening, according to a variety of Internet sites about fitness, ranges between 250 and 272 per hour. That's roughly one Starbucks grande Caffè Latte made with milk, or one Snickers bar. You can get a bit more of a workout if you use heavy equipment during your time in the garden, for example, a rototiller or cutting trees with a chain saw. The calories then add up to around 400 to 405 per hour. But if you love to cook and also appreciate having fresh herbs as well as fruits and vegetables packed with vitamins, minerals, and other nutrients, consider designing and planting a garden and then combine the gardening with cooking for a healthier you. ☺

217 Dance Around Your Kitchen Every Morning as You Make Coffee

Start your day with a little salsa, mambo, cha cha, or your favorite dance steps as you make your way over to measure the coffee, add the water, and turn on the pot. Dance until the coffee is ready, have a cup, and dance some more. Start your fancy footwork in your kitchen and jig throughout your house. If you have to leave for work, dance your way to your dressing room, keep moving while you do your makeup, dance over to pick up your purse, briefcase, and car keys . . . and dance right into the garage. Keep moving and watch the pounds melt away. ☺

218 Buy a Pair of Rollerblades and Skate Your Heart Out

Have you tried skating lately? You can still rent skates and get a workout in a roller skating rink or ice skating facility. Ice skating is particularly fun when done in the winter in an outdoor rink. Roller rinks still offer the young and young-at-heart places to get a workout, complete with music and a light show. Another option is to buy some inline skates designed for skating on paved surfaces such as streets and sidewalks. Inline skates are sleeker and more stable and light-weight than their traditional counterparts. So grab your family or a friend or even your favorite canine for an afternoon outing at the park. Take along a picnic lunch, a bottle of water, and your inline skates. Don't forget to take along some gloves to protect your hands, and pads for your elbows and knees just in case you fall. But don't let the fear of falling keep you from working out and having some fun. Skating particularly works the thighs, calves, and buttock, and when you see the results on your body for doing that type of regular exercise, you'll exercise your facial muscles, too, into a big smile. ☺

219 Take an Eco-Themed Trip to the Rainforest or Other Exotic Locale

Experience sheer exhilaration as you get a workout in an exotic locale. Sign up for a fun-filled eco-tour vacation. Teach your children about ecology and learn some new facts yourself while hiking in nature. You'll burn roughly 544 calories an hour rock or mountain climbing or about 510 per hour if you are just climbing hills with a 10- to 20-pound pack on your back. Head off for the Lapa Rios Ecolodge, a rainforest reserve and wildlife corridor near Costa Rica's Corcovado National Park where you can hike and see spectacular birds and other wildlife. Or travel back in time to discover

ancient Ethiopia and hike with eco-tour guides into the Simien Mountains. If you prefer an exotic locale closer to home, learn about the life of eagles and try a little kayaking on an eagle-watching trip into the wilds of Maryland. The point is to burn calories doing fun activities in a natural setting. ☺

220 Join a Rowing Club

If you like working out with others, join a rowing club. Rowing tones the arms, builds upper body strength, and involves all major muscle groups. Basically, rowing takes two forms. Sculling is when rowers have an oar in each hand. But when the rowers have both hands on one oar, that type of rowing is called sweep rowing. Rowing is a low-impact exercise but does require a degree of agility, grace, and teamwork. Rowing as a team teaches you to work together for

123

maximum effectiveness. The boat advances more quickly when the rowing team members row fast and in unison. So make some new friends, learn the art of rowing, get in a regular workout, and feel good as your body becomes trim and toned. ☺

221 Walk to the Local Market

If there's a grocery store in your neighborhood or a weekend farmer's market, gather together canvas bags or heavy-duty utility bags and head out for a brisk walk to do your grocery shopping. Since you'll be carrying the bags of groceries back home afterwards, you'll want to be sure you can carry what you purchase, in other words, buy only what you need that will fit into a couple of bags. Walking while carrying groceries means you'll be burning a lot more calories than you would driving your car to the store. Plus, it's

better for the environment. Now, that's something to feel good about. ☺

222 Trek the Himalayas

If you've ever wanted to break out of the ordinary routine and taste adventure, trekking might be just the thing to try. Trekking regions of the Himalayas used to be only for adventurers, mountain climbers, and tourists with a liking for remote and exotic destinations. Today, trekking has become a popular pastime for ordinary people with a chunk of time and enough money to get to Nepal or India. It's a good idea for you to join a trekking group if you are a first-time trekker. Trekking, defined generally as walking while carrying a backpack, will take you through lots of different types of terrain if you are walking in regions of the Himalayas. As you hike, you'll burn lots of calories. Your muscles will become firmer and stronger and you'll begin to feel mental, spiritual, and physical renewal. Read up on trekking; give it a try. ☺

223 Build a House with Habitat for Humanity

Swing a hammer, carry some lumber, and otherwise help build a home for a poor family if this appeals to your social conscience. Habitat for Humanity is a nonprofit organization that works in tandem with volunteers in communities worldwide to build houses for low-income people. Former president Jimmy Carter and his wife spend a week every year swinging hammers to help erect affordable shelter for the poor on behalf of Habitat for Humanity. If you believe that you could be doing more to help the less fortunate, then grab your hammer, go out, and work up a sweat with people like yourself working with Habitat for Humanity. ☺

CHAPTER 13

Spend Deliriously Happy Hours on a Hobby

224 Take a Stained Glass Class

Learn the art and craft of creating a beautiful piece of a stained glass by signing up for a hands-on class. A class can provide you with an in-depth exploration of types of glass production, materials needed for a project, the design work of a window or panel, and other ingredients necessary to produce a stained glass project. While your instructor will be able to teach you the basics, it is often through hands-on work that you gain a comprehensive understanding of the art form. You'll meet new people in your stained glass class and, who knows, one or more of them might become friends with whom you can spend many happy hours together creating works of art. In time, you might even choose to organize a show, establish an art collective, or sell your creations through word of mouth. ☺

225 Create Jewelry with Beads

Beading has increased in popularity in recent years and is considered by many to be not only a high art form but also a way to earn some extra bucks. Already, there are several magazines devoted to beading and columns about beading in others. Whether you want to create beaded jewelry or works of art, you'll soon discover that time seems to fly as you discover beads in assorted styles, shapes, colors, and textures; decide on the optimum way to use them; and then create beautiful earrings, chokers, bracelets, pins, and necklaces. To find beads, visit a bead shop, department stores, and art and crafts outlets. Have fun making your distinctive pieces as gifts for birthdays and other celebratory occasions, showing them in galleries, or selling them in stores or online. ☺

226 Make a Piece of Pottery

Maybe you, like a lot of other people, made mud pies as a child. Discover what the ancients knew about the warm, fuzzy feelings you get working with your hands to produce a piece of pottery. Spend some happy hours pinching off a ball of clay, centering it on a potter's wheel, shaping it, firing out the impurities, glazing it, and then firing it again to affix the glaze. You will need access to clay, the wheel, and a kiln that can heat at high temperatures (for example, around 1700°F). A pottery class can provide all those essential items along with instruction and coaching. Or, you could purchase the type of clay that can be fired in your own oven at lower temperatures and make some nifty beads to string. See *www.howtomakepottery.com*. ☺

227 Join an Association Devoted to Your Hobby

You know you love working on your hobby. Whatever your hobby is, there's undoubtedly a professional association representing it. To find yours, type the name of your hobby into your computer browser and see what it lists. Or, go to *www.hobby.org*, where you will discover the hottest new crafts and hobbies in the global marketplace. For example, scrapbooking, quilting and needlecrafts, art, and framing top the list today. The association(s) for your hobby might host annual competitions, produce a magazine, or provide grants or scholarships so that deserving individuals can learn more about their favorite hobby. ☺

Spend Deliriously Happy Hours on a Hobby

228 Teach a Cooking Class in Your Kitchen

Perhaps you like to cook, have some culinary expertise, and some great recipes for dishes such as a Jewish poppy seed mandlebrot (biscotti), an Indian fish curry, a paella that even Spaniards love, a fried chicken made from a recipe that your Southern great-grandmother passed on, or some other tantalizing taste treat. Start a cooking class in your kitchen. Alternatively, reserve another facility and step into the role of teacher. Make sure you have all the pieces of equipment and utensils that you'll need. Decide on a theme for your class—maybe quick and easy desserts, Italian pasta dishes, Indian curries, or sandwiches and pastries for high tea. Type your recipes for each student and make sure that you prepare and cook the long dishes at the beginning of the class and dishes that need less prep and cooking time at the end. Have fun teaching and sharing your passion for food with others. ☺

229 Host a Quilting Party

Quilting is so much fun that many quilters have quilting parties to enjoy the camaraderie of friends and to finish their own quilts or to join with other quilters to sew a project for a charitable cause. Many people equate quilt making with the Pennsylvania Dutch Amish or the Appalachian people. Amish quilts, especially the antique quilts, are of the highest-quality construction, but there are many other types of quilts that require less exacting and demanding skill to make. For example, you can make a crazy quilt from pieces of leftover fabric. Or you can contribute a square to someone else's quilt (this is the way the AIDS quilt is constructed). Buy a quilting how-to book, take a class, or just dive in and do it. Then invite your friends who sew to a quilting party. It's never too early or late to work on quilts for holiday gift giving. ☺

hobby, you and your family can visit museums, read books about your models, and plan family vacations to places where that model made history. ☺

 230 Build a Model Airplane, Train, or Ship

As a child, did you ever play with little models of World War II fighter planes and ships or a miniature train set up on tracks with it's own little village? If you did, you probably have some fond memories of that time. There are many advantages to resuming that activity now that you are an adult. For example, you can build a plane, ship, or train alone and enjoy some worry-free, downtime. Or, you can spend some quality time working on a favorite model project with a young family member and share with him or her some of the history behind that model. Additionally, if you really get into that

231 Promote Yourself and Your Projects

When you feel passionate about your hobby, whether it is freehand painting of murals on the walls of children's rooms, sculpting bowls from driftwood, or making cigar box shrines, tell your friends and other hobby enthusiasts about your latest project. Word gets around. You may attract people who want to see your projects, perhaps even purchase your services or product. Post digital photos of your creations on your social networking sites or photo sharing sites. You never know what opportunities may come your way when you put aside false modesty and instead promote yourself and your passion for your particular hobby. ☺

232 List Four Ways Your Hobby Could Become a Fundraiser

Consider your hobby as a way to raise funds for your favorite cause. Let's say you paint wooden ornaments and tie them with red ribbon to hang on Christmas trees. You fashion napkin rings out of Christmas dried floral items, wire, and floral tape. Or, you make wind chimes out of spoons or little Mexican crosses. You make birdhouses, sew place-mats, or breed orchids. Think of four or more ways you could spin off your hobby into fundraising. For example, you could:

- Host or participate in a holiday boutique
- Approach a hospital to organize a silent auction to purchase a piece of equipment
- Sell your item through your own website
- Auction your items on an online auction site and donate the proceeds ☺

233 Attend Hobby Trade Shows

When you feel passionate about your hobby, nothing gets your creative juices flowing like attending a convention or a trade show. From scrap-booking to cooking, quilting, designing (everything from furniture and boats to clothing), and collecting (wine, coins, stamps, sports or movie memorabilia, religious items, dishware, glassware, or virtually any-thing), you'll likely find a trade show for it. Locate one for your hobby by searching the Internet or perusing magazines and newsletters for enthusiasts who share your passion about your particular hobby and for discovering the latest and greatest innovations or products. Many industry trade shows and conventions are for wholesale buyers only, but some do welcome hobbyists and the general public. ☺

 ## 234 Search the Internet to Find Lower Material Costs

Hobbies can be an expensive enterprise. Take photography, for example. Cameras and lenses can cost a small fortune. Oil painters have a similar problem if they want high-quality paint and premium canvases. But if you have time and persistence, you can often find items you need for your hobby at competitive prices on the Internet. Teaming up with others who share your interest in a particular hobby can sometimes help you get a better price because you can buy in bulk. Search for those good deals and share them with your friends and colleagues. Buy two for one when possible, such as tubes of oil paint or bags of beads, and look for other ways to reduce your cost of buying hobby materials. ☺

235 Invite a Dozen Friends for a Wine Tasting

If you and your friends enjoy the occasional glass of wine, consider forming a club. Host monthly blind tastings and share information about oenology or the science of viniculture. Before each meeting, decide on one type of wine you will taste that session, for example, pinots, cabernet sauvignons, burgundies, chardonnays, sauvignon blancs, zinfandels, or something different. Have each person bring a bottle of the selected wine and one appetizer to share with everyone. Place each bottle in a paper bag with a number. Put out pencils and note cards so guests can write remarks about each numbered bottle they taste. You might even suggest a trip together to Napa or other wine region to visit the wineries and taste some great wine. Learn to pair wines with good food and for a heightened culinary experience. ☺

236 Take Your Watercolors on Vacation and Paint Places You See

If you like to dabble in watercolor, take your paints with you on your next vacation. You'll also need paper, a tablet, a stack of cards made for watercolor painting, or a sketch/paint book. When you return home from your sojourns into the world, you'll enjoy looking at your paintings and remembering the places you visited. You'll probably remember more details about your vacation travels long after your trip is over. You might even decide to frame a few of your works of art for yourself or as gifts for others. ☺

237 Photograph the Great Cities of Europe

Indulge your interest in photography by planning your own photo junket to Europe's most beautiful and historic cities. These days, cameras come in all sizes and weights, so there's no reason not to take one or more of them along. Many of the newest digital models enable you to take professional-quality photos in a rapid sequence. All you need to do is point and click. Once you have taken a variety of stunningly beautiful pictures of Paris, London, Prague, and other legendary cities, simply remove the camera chip and slip it into your computer. E-mail them to your family and friends who'll think you are simply amazing. And, of course, you are. ☺

238 Build a Kit Car with a Friend

If you are a budding Henry Ford and you love tinkering with automobiles, take your hobby to a new level. Enlist the help of a friend and build your own vehicle from a car kit. Be aware of the fact that some kits may supply many, but not necessarily all, of the parts and materials that you will need to complete the project. An engine, for example, may have to be harvested from another automobile in a junkyard or acquired from an online source if it is not included in your kit. Some of the best-known kit cars are the Lotus 7 and the AC Cobra. In fact, the manufacturer of Lotus started out as a maker of kit cars. But you probably already knew that, didn't you? ☺

239 Show Off Your Baking Skills at a Bake Sale or County Fair

You know your way around the kitchen and you've experimented with a recipe or two to make them even tastier. Organize or participate in a local bake sale. Or, this summer head off with your special culinary creation to your county fair. Get some validation for your incredible baking skills. Wouldn't it be great to be able to say your razmadoodle pie was judged the best in your entire county? Sure it would. And that blue ribbon would give you bragging rights for years to come. And it's not beyond possibility that magazine editors, ingredient producers, and organizers of national bake-off competitions might call on you with invitations for you to share your secrets. You might want to start practicing your Food Network smile. ☺

Spend Deliriously Happy Hours on a Hobby

240 Start a Collection

What kinds of things do you find yourself drawn to at flea markets, country fairs, white elephant sales, auctions, recycle shops, roadside sales, and in long-forgotten boxes in attics and basements? One of the easiest ways to start a collection is by acquiring something that attracts you, perhaps because of its historical significance, beauty, or value. Whether it's amber jewelry, salt and pepper shaker sets from the turn of the century, furniture with hammered tin doors, old postcards, Victorian serving utensils, or something else that captures your fancy, use it to start a collection. Set a budget for your collection, make space in your home for it, expand what you know about your collectible, and network with others who buy and sell that item. Then spend many happy hours searching for items to add to your collection. ☺

241 Invent Something

Do your creative juices start to flow the instant you see something new and immediately have an idea for making it even more functional or efficient? Do you enjoy pondering the way things work? Do you like exercising your brain about innovative ways of doing things? You may have that creative spark that all inventors share. Just tinkering around with your product idea, making drawings or notes, and even naming it can bring you happiness. Improve upon an existing product or develop a totally new one. Find a niche in the marketplace, something that is needed but doesn't yet exist. That is the way thousands of products came to be produced. The right invention could take you from Main Street to Easy Street. ☺

CHAPTER 14

Stay Happy When Dealing with Adversaries

242 Make a List of Your Adversary's Strength and Weaknesses

You've heard the old adage that knowledge is power. Of course, the converse of that would state that lack of knowledge is weakness. Why do you think high-ranking political candidates hire advisors to research strengths and weaknesses of their adversaries? Politicians understand that to win elections they have to know what's bad and good about their opponents as well as how to spin that information to sway public opinion before people cast their ballots. That strategy that works so well in the political process and in the business world can work for you. List everything you know about your adversary's strengths and weaknesses. Add to the information you don't know by doing more research. You'll feel happier and more empowered when you know your opponent as well as a close family member. ☺

243 Invite Your Adversary to Coffee

What if you owned a vintage dress shop four doors from another second-hand dress store that just opened? Would you sit down and meet with the new owner if the knowledge you gained from the meeting helped you better compete? It might be a good idea. Suggest having coffee as a way to open dialogue between you. Use the time to see where ideologies between the two of you dovetail or depart. Actively listen and repeat what you think your adversary just said. You may discover discrepancies between what was actually said and what you thought was stated. See if you can find common ground. Is there a way you might team up to bring more business into both stores? Find win-win scenarios that might serve you both well. ☺

244 Ask Competitors or Adversaries to Name Their Issues

What if a top competitor could become an ally, perhaps even a partner, if you could just deal with the issues that keep you apart? Unless you seek to know and understand your competitors' issues, you won't have a clue about how to narrow the gap in your opposing viewpoints. What if you desire to acquire a company that is competing with yours for market share and that company doesn't want to be acquired? You must find out why the company doesn't wish to be acquired, how long it could hold out, and if it is looking at partnerships with other companies. If you do manage the acquisition, getting all the issues on the table and dealing with them can pave the way for a smoother, happier transition. ☺

245 Ensure that You Understand Your Adversary's Position

When you are faced with having to negotiate a dispute, it's a good idea to first thoroughly understand your adversary's position. Sun Tzu stated in his book from the sixth century B.C., *The Art of War*, that when you know both yourself and your enemy then victory will not stand in doubt. Invite your adversary to tell you about his point of view. Then articulate your understanding of what he has told you. Ask him for suggestions on how to resolve the dispute. You then will be in the optimal position for offering your own ideas and, hopefully, come to some resolution with the other party. ☺

Stay Happy When Dealing with Adversaries

246 Find Common Ground on One or More Points

Perhaps you have gotten nowhere in your debate with a colleague, business rival, or relative. Sometimes all you can do is tell the other person that you understand her position but that you respectfully disagree. Still, try to find one or more items or ideas on which you can agree and use those as points of departure for a discussion. When you are engaged, express your point of view in language that is neither inflammatory nor confrontational. Try to keep your voice calm and focus on the topic, rather than on the person's character, values, or ethics. Ultimately, you may simply agree to continue the dialogue and agree to disagree. ☺

247 Make a Self-Deprecating Joke to Diffuse Hostility

You have already learned that humor can lift your mood, shift your mental or physical fatigue, strengthen your immune system, and provide resilience, but here's another great thing about humor: You can use it to diffuse hostility. When you use self-deprecating humor or poke fun at yourself, you can get relief in tense or hostile situations. Your sense of humor and laughter literally channels your fear of hostility and potential aggression into a lighter, less fearful state of mind. ☺

248 Use Five of Your Adversary's Favorite Words to Respond to His Complaints

People like to hear themselves talk, and they like to talk about themselves the most. In an adversarial situation, you can use a person's self-infatuation to your advantage. The language they use will be peppered with their favorite words or expressions. Listen closely enough to catch them. If you remain reasonable and calm, you will be in a better position to respond rationally, using their words to phrase your argument, than if you allow yourself to get all worked up emotionally. Using facts and logic, you win arguments by proving someone wrong, not by proving yourself right. ☺

 249 Use Three Anger Management Techniques to Deal with Hostility

If you don't already know some anger management techniques, try three or more of the following the next time you must deal with someone's hostility. Breathe deeply. Try to understand your adversary's point of view. Avoid a knee-jerk reaction or allowing anger to overshadow rational thoughts. Know your triggers or hot buttons and change your actions or direction as soon as you recognize a trigger. Assertively communicate what you feel in response to what's being said or what's going on in your environment. Lower or eliminate expectations. Anger can be triggered when an expectation isn't met. Remove yourself from the situation. Accept and forgive, if you can, because anger turned into resentment hurts you more than it does the person who offended you. ☺

 250 Think of a Contingency Plan if Resolution Fails

You've been fighting for weeks and resolution does not appear to be on the horizon. Consider the following: money is tight, your wife got laid off from her job, and both of your children need braces. You refuse to make the sacrifice your wife wants, that is, give up your San Francisco Giant season tickets. She says you can still go to some of the games, but forget sitting in that luxury box. It's time for you to figure out some contingency possibilities. You could sell your motorcycle that is just sitting in the garage, or find another way to free up the money needed for the braces and to make up the difference between your wife's unemployment check and what her salary used to be. Chances are, when you bring some alternative options to the table, rational negotiations between you can be resumed. ☺

251 Walk Away if That's Your Only Option

If it becomes apparent anytime during your confrontation with an adversary that the situation is moving out of control and may even become violent, walk away. Your adversary cannot continue the battle without you. As you walk, use breathing and counting techniques to feel calmer. Ask yourself why you are angry, what was the hot button your opponent pushed? How did things escalate to the point where they were getting out of hand? Be truthful with yourself about your role in the escalation. Whether it is your wife, your boss, or a colleague, think about what you will say to your adversary when you next face him or her. You don't want to say anything that you will later regret. ☺

252 State Unequivocally Your Desire for Understanding

You may gain valuable insights and possibly a breakthrough with your adversary by taking anger's opposing position of tenderness and understanding. If talking about what you are feeling or expressing your anger doesn't completely diffuse it, try some mind-body techniques like meditation. Then when you are calmer, approach your husband, boss, friend, relative, colleague, competitor, or whoever is your adversary with a clear statement of desire to work through the seeming impasse. Make it absolutely clear that you desire understanding and that you will do whatever it takes to reach a resolution. ☺

 253 Ask for Three Specific Ideas to Resolve the Conflict

You don't have to do all the work. Ask your adversary to come up with three ideas to resolve the conflict that you two are facing. Simultaneously, you can be brainstorming three ideas as well. With six ideas to discuss, the balance of power will be moving back and forth between you. Also, when you move out of your old entrenched positions to new territory where you explore ideas for solutions, you both are shifting the paradigm that kept you entrenched and stuck. You move away from acting out on negative triggers and instead move onto positive ground. ☺

254 Offer Adversaries Something They Want or Need

Many times, negotiating a solution that is acceptable to all parties means each side must give up something. For example, your boss wants a report completed by the end of the workday on Friday. It is past quitting time on Thursday and you are already late for your child's parent-teacher's conference. As you think about the mountains you will have to move in order to give her what she wants, you feel your anger building to the boiling point. What can you do? First, think about what your boss wants and why she chose to give the assignment to you. Perhaps she has more confidence in you than anyone else. Ask to have the day off so that you can work on the report at home without meetings, phone calls, and other interruptions. She'll have to do without you for the day if you are to deliver the report by the close of business. ☺

255 Involve a Mediator, Negotiator, or Closer for Impasses

There are occasions in life when you might need a mediator or otherwise independent third party to negotiate a resolution to an impasse. Whether it's a divorce or a dispute with a business partner, using a mediator to negotiate the settlement can oftentimes be a lot cheaper and

quicker than involving a lawyer, especially if the dispute is fairly straightforward. If you want to remain on good terms with your adversary because you will continue having a relationship with that person (such as a relative, coworker, landlord, or neighbor), then mediation to quickly solve the dispute will prove invaluable. ☺

256 Make a Note Each Time Your Opponent Budges from His Position

Having a notepad and pen with you isn't just for formal debates. Make a mental note when you detect a shift, however slight, in your opponent's position, and write it down along with date, time, and circumstances when the shift occurred. Then use it to bolster your argument that his position is not absolute. For example, your boss might not feel you need a raise, but you do. You ask him for it. He says not now. You tell him it can even be a modest amount, but he still says no. The next month, you ask again and he says unlikely, but that he'll think about it. That's not the same as the absolute no you heard earlier. Months later, you ask again and he tells you it is likely you'll get the raise when there's a new fiscal budget. When that new budget comes through, you can approach your boss and state your case, using your notes to show him his last comment. Doing so may help you leverage your position for achieving a positive outcome. ☺

257 Remind Yourself Before Negotiations That the Answer Is No Until You Ask

You want something from someone but are anxious about asking for it. Never approach a negotiation with the mindset that you will not get what you seek. Instead, remember that you have to first mentally claim what you want. You also have to seek it and ask for it believing that you will get something and possibly everything you ask for. Once you have affirmed to your angels, wife, boss, competitor, children, and friends, for example, exactly what it is you want, you put yourself into a positive mindset for believing that you will actually receive it. You can let go of the anxiety and feel positive and hopeful. ☺

258 Remind Yourself That Happiness Is a Journey

If you look back over the past week and discover that you had moments of happiness, albeit fleeting ones, but moments of stress, anxiety, frustration, exasperation, sadness, resentment, jealousy, impatience, worry, concern, anger, and fear dominated, grab a cup of your favorite tea, put your feet up, and consider this: happy isn't something that you feel only after you've accomplished everything you want to achieve in life. Nope. It's available to you during every step of the journey. But you make the choice of whether or not you experience it. ☺

259 Spend Twenty Minutes Writing in Your Journal about Unity in Diversity

Your adversaries might express different points of view and approaches to life than you do, but in reality, they really aren't that different from you. Try to develop empathy for your adversary. Imagine being inside his skin, understanding (to the degree you can imagine) his life experience, and seeing the world through his eyes. You might discover that there is more that connects you than separates you. Read the universal declaration of human rights at *www.un.org /Overview/rights.html*. Then write in your journal about unity in diversity. Permit your writing to become a lens for seeing through to underlying truths. ☺

CHAPTER 15

Let Animals Bring Happiness into Your Life

260 Offer to Pet Sit for Someone for a Weekend

A great way to decide on whether or not to get a pet is to offer to pet sit for a friend. It's a good idea to care for the animal in its own environment rather than in your home because a puppy, for example, that likes to chew on things may ruin your favorite book, table leg, or shoes. But you can learn from pet sitting. You might discover that a guinea pig is not the right pet for you because of its nocturnal nature. An iguana might not move enough, and a parrot could show itself to be too possessive or talkative. But if you friend's pet is a dog, there's a good chance you will spend a happy weekend. Discover what many pet owners have learned, that their pets bring them much fun and happiness. ☺

261 Perform a Cost Analysis for Pet Ownership Before You Get One

If you want to be a happy pet owner, then figure out how much that lovable little critter is going to cost you before you adopt him. Some surprises aren't so nice. You want to be sure that your budget can support the cost of such items as pet food (and treats and supplements), flea control products, veterinarian visits, annual shots, spaying, and city registrations (some communities require that register your pet and pay a fee). Once you know that you can afford your pet, then go ahead and welcome that little guy or gal into your life and expect to spend many happy hours enjoying your pet. ☺

262 Adopt a Rescued Animal

Sadly, not all dogs and cats brought into this world are guaranteed either a happy or a long life. And just because someone owns an animal does not guarantee they will properly care for it. Animal shelters all over America often have more animals than they can care for, meaning that some animals' lives will end there. You can make a difference by adopting a pet from a shelter. ☺

263 Read a Book about the Personality of Your Chosen Pet

You know you want a dog, but if you want to be happy and stay sane, don't get a dog just because it is adorable and friendly. Take the time to read a little about the various dog breeds. As for dogs of mixed breeds that you might find at a shelter, the shelter staff can most likely provide information about the dog's temperament. Whether purebred or mixed breed, some animals require more patience, understanding, and training than others. Of course, you will love your pet, but some of the things you might consider include whether or not it is:

- Aggressive toward other dogs
- Independent and stubborn
- Affectionate and good with children
- Territorial
- Likes to dig
- Barks a lot ☺

264 Plan and Host a Monthly Party for Pet Owners and Their Animals

You love outings with your dog so why not plan a dog party? Since a gathering of pet owners

Let Animals Bring Happiness into Your Life

and their animals might not work so well for cats, iguanas, or turtles, you might want to stick to inviting only owners of dogs. Plan to host the outing at a local park, where the dogs can run and catch Frisbees and owners, when they are tired, can hang out in the shade and visit. Take along water and doggie treats for the canines and don't forget some little snacks for the pet owners. You want the day to be pleasurable for all who attend. ☺

265 Enroll in a Pet Training/Obedience Class

A happy pet owner is someone whose pet follows commands. You don't want your animal running off and not returning when you call her name. If your pet behaves like a rascal, for example, gets aggressive around other dogs, snarls threateningly at your friends or children, or doesn't follow your commands, causing you to fear for the animal's safety, it may be time to enroll in a dog training or obedience class. Perhaps all you need is a little refresher for the two of you to restore your peace of mind. ☺

266 Make Your Pet's Exercise Period Part of Your Regular Routine

Exercise is a very important part of keeping your dog mentally and physically healthy. Regular exercise keeps your animal trim, agile, limber, and mentally alert. Physical exercise improves his joint health as well. Take him to the dog park where he can play with other dogs, too, because dog experts say it is good for his socialization skills. If your dog belongs to one of the larger dog breeds like Labrador or German Shepherd, leaving him in your back yard does not guarantee that he will exercise on his own. Take the time to exercise together as part of your daily routine. Think of it as happy bonding. ☺

267 Schedule Your New Pet for an Immediate Veterinarian Visit

By sixteen weeks, your little cat or dog should have already received his core vaccinations. After that, regular visits to the veterinarian can ensure that your pet will have optimal health. When a problem arises, the vet usually can catch and deal with it before it develops into a major medical issue. So don't wait to make that initial appointment to have the vet check over your new pet. And, if it's been a while since you've had your other pets checked, make appointments for them as well. To ensure that you don't forget to ask about something, write down discussion points for the visit, including your pet's exposure to poisons, toxins, and communicable diseases. In addition, note any changes in sleep, diet, temperament, as well as exposures to ticks and fleas. When you know your pet is healthy, you can simply relax and enjoy him. ☺

268 Find a Good Recipe and Make Homemade Dog Biscuits

Instead of buying dog biscuits or other doggie treats, consider making some healthy treats. Look for recipes on the Internet (there are hundreds) or make up your own using natural ingredients including wholesome and healthy grains, vegetables, and proteins. Just like humans, dogs like foods that taste good. Remember to avoid chocolate and raw meat as well as artificial ingredients and

Let Animals Bring Happiness into Your Life

additives that might cause illness or even death to some dogs. You'll feel better knowing that your dog is healthy and happy. ☺

269 Examine Your Pet Each Day for Signs of Injury or Ill Health

Some animal caregivers and veterinarians, too, advocate a regular daily examination of your pet for early signs of ill health or a recent injury. An excellent time to check your dog, for example, might be right after an exercise period when she has been running with you along the beach, on a track, or through a park. Tell your vet if your cat or dog walks with a different gait than usual, suddenly has the sniffles, or is constantly licking a particular area. Also, notice any changes in appetite, sleep patterns, or a desire to play as these can be warning signs of illness or injury.

Keep your pet healthy and she'll reward you with her devotion and love. ☺

270 Get Your Pet Spayed

Spay your pet. The animal shelters across America and the Humane Society advocate it because the numbers of homeless dogs and cats has reached epidemic proportions in the United States, and millions of those animals must be euthanized. Before an animal can be adopted, many centers require them to be neutered or spayed. There are a number of low-cost, affordable programs for spaying. And contrary to what some people believe, spaying does not make your animal fat and lazy, although it can make a pet more docile and get rid of his desire to roam. Animals get fat from a bad diet or overeating and not exercising enough. For more information, see www.adoptapet.com/public/spay_and_neuter/. Happier pets make for happier owners. ☺

271 Volunteer at an Animal Shelter

Volunteer your free time at your local animal shelter. You will be a volunteer parent to a lonely, even possibly abandoned or abused, animal. You may be asked to help in various ways, including transporting animals to their veterinarian appointments, participating in community activities that foster animal adoptions, educating the public about the need for humane treatment of animals, cleaning out animal cages, and reuniting lost pets with their owners, to name a few. For animal lovers, such work can not only be satisfying, it can give meaning and purpose to their lives. And those are vital elements of life satisfaction and happiness. ☺

272 Join a Local Animal Rescue Group

As a rescuer, you will be contacted by a shelter or a rescue organization when volunteer help is needed. Helping creatures that cannot help themselves can give your life purpose. Whether it is a beached dolphin or whale, or a bird of prey such as a falcon or an eagle with a broken wing, you and the other rescue team members may be able to give that animal another chance to live out its life in the wild. Even if you cannot volunteer time, you can make a monetary donation or contribute items on a local shelter's wish list. A California shelter has on its wish list peanut butter, plastic bags, bath towels, pet carriers (all sizes for all kinds of pets), and good-quality canned dog and puppy food, for example. See a need and fill it. The resulting good feelings are yours to keep. ☺

Let Animals Bring Happiness into Your Life

273 Take Your Pet on Day Trips or Vacation

Whenever you can steal away for a little rest and relaxation, think about taking along your pet. There are numerous hotels and RV parks that now welcome pet owners. You might find one in your local area or desired vacation destination by searching *www.dogfriendly.com* or *www.pet-friendly-hotels.net* or checking out various books and guides for day, weekend, or longer trips If you hesitate to take your pet along on a vacation because of her tendency to suffer canine motion sickness, talk with your veterinarian to learn about new ways of dealing with that issue. Nondrowsy drugs for motion sickness are available for dogs. And, you can work with your dog on shorter outings to acclimate her for a longer trip. Your pet will appreciate the change of scenery as much as you. ☺

274 Make a Disaster To-Do List That Ensures the Safety of Your Pet

Your family perhaps already knows the safety procedures and evacuation plan in the event of a disaster such as a hurricane, tornado, fire, or flood. But have you figured out the plan to ensure the safety of your pet? If not, call a family meeting to discuss evacuating the animals. Each year, animals perish in unexpected natural disasters. When Hurricane Katrina struck, volunteers were needed to rescue thousands of animals, many of whom perished. During that crisis, an untold number of pets waited weeks for owners to return or for help to arrive and, in many cases, help never came. A good, solid plan for your pet's safety means you won't fail him when such a crisis hits. ☺

275 Brush Your Dog or Cat's Teeth and Get Dental Exams

Dogs and cats can suffer tooth decay, gum infection, and even tooth loss. In animals, the pain of tooth decay and gum disease can be excruciating and protracted. If you aren't already ensuring that your pet gets regular dental exams and brushing her teeth, begin soon because the possibility of decay and infection is more likely if you disregard this important task. An animal can't tell you why she isn't eating, why she's losing weight, why she's got terrible bad breath (could be a digestive problem), or even starving to death, so it's up to you to ensure she can eat and get the nutrition she needs. As her owner, your responsibility is to ensure she gets to live a healthy and happy life. ☺

276 Set Aside One Day Each Week to Clean Your Pet's Cage

Whether your pet is a small animal or a bird, you'll want to keep your pet's cage clean. A clean cage provides a healthy environment and contributes to the well-being of your pet. It also means the cage and its contents won't be a source of noxious odors. Remember to wear gloves to protect against the dust of droppings that can cause illness. Soap and water is usually sufficient for cleaning a cage, even if it has lots of crevices and surfaces. Your pet is more likely to be healthy living in a clean environment, so do your part to contribute to his longevity and ensure your own peace of mind. ☺

Donate an Hour or Two Each Week to Work at an Equine Therapy Center

Consider volunteering at your local equine therapy center. Horses and kids are able to forge bonds in special ways; equine centers with a focus on education or offering therapy modalities have become a vital source to help at-risk kids make good choices, and provide positive experiences for children with life-threatening illnesses. Some centers focus on children and teen learning, emotional growth, and mental health. Other centers focus on riding as therapy for a physically challenged child. Help a child succeed. If you love working and caring for horses, consider a generous weekly donation of your time at an equine center near you. ☺

CHAPTER 16

Plan Several Happy Celebrations During the Year

278 Plan Your Own Birthday Bash

Instead of having the usual dinner with the lover, spouse, or relatives, why not plan an exhilarating birthday bash that you'll never forget. Perhaps you are turning thirty and want to fly to London to shop at Harrods and then go to the theater district to see a play. What are you waiting for? Book the reservations. You're only thirty once. Or, perhaps you're turning forty and are thinking about doing a vision quest. Get in your jeep and head to the desert. Maybe this is your big five-o year and you've always wanted to skydive. Get on down to your local airport and find out what's involved. Whatever you do, do it your way and enjoy every minute of it. ☺

279 Reserve the Clubhouse and Celebrate a Great Golf Game

You played that game of golf as if you were Tiger Woods. So why not milk that event for the greatest amount of happiness possible? Turn that exhilarating win into an excuse to celebrate with your golfing buddies, family members, and friends. Reserve the party room at the clubhouse. Bring in a cake decorated with a golfing theme. Ask someone to make your favorite punch. Relive every minute of that game as you explain the high and low moments of that day. It's your party and everyone there has come to honor you and your skill as a golfer. That game is surely destined for family storytelling for years to come, so don't hesitate to invite questions. Include all the details in your answers and feel the joy again. ☺

280 Invite Wine Tasting Club Members to a Formal Christmas Party

How often do you get to dress up in formal attire? If you love wearing silk or satin, getting your hair and nails done, and feeling the excitement of a big day, host a formal holiday gathering for your wine club members. Make the event a blind tasting of champagne and sparkling wines from French and American vineyards. Ask members to bring appetizers that pair nicely with the beverages and to also bring a wrapped gift for either a boy or a girl. The day after your party, take the donated gifts to a charity or a local fire department to distribute to low-income families with children. ☺

281 Order Beer, Beans, and Burritos for a Cinco de Mayo Party

Get in the spirit of Cinco de Mayo, held May 5th each year. The day marks the triumph of the Mexican militia over the French army in the 1862 Battle of Puebla in the Mexican state of Puebla. The holiday is celebrated in areas of the United States where there are large Hispanic populations, such as the U.S. border with Mexico, California, and Texas. Throw some colorful Mexican cotton blankets on the table, set out some green cacti, red chili peppers, and miniature sombreros. Place a grouping of candles, each in a terra cotta pot in the center of your table. Then, make some traditional Mexican foods and serve with margaritas or just order in some beans, burritos, and beers. Invite your neighbors and friends over to celebrate. ☺

Plan Several Happy Celebrations During the Year

282 Dress in Attire from Hollywood's Heyday and Host an Oscar Night Event

If it's March and you are looking for an excuse to break the monotony of your winter doldrums, get into the party spirit with an Oscar bash. Find out what night the film industry will be hosting its annual Academy Award celebrations, and schedule a party on that night. Some film buffs say that Hollywood's film industry was in its heyday in the 1930s and 1940s. Ask everyone to dress in attire that reflects that golden time in filmmaking. Offer appetizers and drinks and pass around cards asking your guests to pick the nominees for best actress and actor, screenplay, and picture. Enjoy the televised Academy Awards celebration and cheer on your picks for the winning actor, actress, picture, and script. ☺

283 Make a Roman Honey Cake for an Engagement Announcement

If you are looking for a special kind of cake to make for an engagement party, consider a medieval honey cake. The taste of honey, a natural sweetener, depends on the part of the world where it is produced. It takes its flavor from the flower nectar the bees gather. Mead or ale made with honey has been around for thousands of years and was especially loved by the Romans, Greeks, and Jews. In fact, those three cultures all have a version of the ancient honey cake. Many Jewish cooks prepare a honey cake for Rosh Hashanah, the Jewish New Year. It symbolizes a wish for all good things and sweetness in the coming year. That sort of wish is also appropriate for an engagement announcement. For a historical Roman honey cake recipe, go to *www.history.uk.com/recipes/index.php?archives=10*. ☺

284 Create a Guest List and Include Five Funny People

Laughter is good for your health and longevity, and comedy adds fun and frivolity to any gathering. So, the next time you're thinking of throwing a party, kick up your happiness quotient a notch or two and make sure that your guest list includes some people with a natural sense of humor. Give your comedic friends free reign to do a little standup work or try out some new material. Make sure they know ahead of time that you will have a receptive audience who enjoys a good laugh. Then join in the fun; laugh until your muscles hurt. ☺

285 Plan a Woodstock Event in a Pasture and Wear Tie-Dye

If you are looking for theme party ideas, consider the party at Woodstock. You remember Woodstock, that gathering of sixties-era rock 'n roll musicians and their fans who camped out for a weekend in Max Yasgur's 600-acre field in New York? The 1969 event has long been linked to the hedonism of hippies and the excesses of that decade. Plan a little counterculture bash of your own in a pasture. Don't have a pasture? Try the back yard. No problem getting the musicians either. Just put on CDs of the music of Jimi Hendrix, Janis Joplin, Joan Baez, Grateful Dead, Richie Havens, Ravi Shankar, and others who performed that weekend. Tell your guests to wear their favorite tie-dye and plan to have a blast. ☺

286 Play One or More Icebreaker Games at Your Next Party

Icebreaker games are intended to help you and your guests quickly break down barriers to conversation, facilitate introductions, and get people animated and focused on having fun. In the Who Am I game, for example, each guest writes the name of a famous person onto a self-stick sheet of note paper and affixes it on someone's back. That person has to ask questions until he discovers the identity of the person whose name is on his back. There are many icebreaker games you can play, depending on the size of your party. Especially helpful in easing introductions of strangers to each other, icebreakers get the fun started and keep it going until the party is over. ☺

287 Enlist a Neighbor to Help You Plan Your Street's July Fourth Party

One way to get your neighbors to come out of their houses and socialize a little is to plan an Independence Day street party for the families on your street. Mention the holiday and most people think of parades, fireworks, and outdoor cooking as well as the colors of red, white, and blue. If you plan far enough ahead, you can ask your local police department to allow you and your neighbors to rope off your street to through traffic on that day. Then get the children excited about having their own parade with wagons, trikes, and bikes. Hold a Fourth of July cake bakeoff. Plan games for different age groups at opposite ends of the street and use the middle for barbeque pits and lawn furniture for your outdoor meal. It will be a memorable Fourth, so plan on taking lots of pictures to trigger happy memories years from now. ☺

 288 Hang Streamers in Primary Colors to Create an Energetic Party Mood

Nothing says "party" like colored streamers. Red, blue, and yellow are the primary colors of the color wheel, and from those three, all other colors, except for white, can be made. The primary colors are not just for children's parties. They energize any festive occasion. Use the colors in decorations or your party furniture. Go wild with color the way the 1980s Milan-based designer group Memphis did when they created wild, whimsical, and nonsensical furniture, such as a tomato-red couch with blue or yellow legs. Break free. Go bold. Be happy doing it. ☺

289 Choose Music That Makes People Want to Dance

If you are like most people, you like a lively party over one that's dull and boring. Dance music can get people out of their chairs and off the barstools, window seats, and benches onto the dance floor. Music has drawn people from sitting positions to moving and swaying upright for thousands of years. And it really doesn't matter if the music derives from clapping sticks together or playing CDs. When your guests are on their feet, stomping to some backbeats, you just naturally feel happy knowing that you helped them have a good time. ☺

290 Write a Notable Fact for Each Guest on Her Party Name Tag

You enjoy singing the praises of your friends' accomplishments and probably know more about the people you invite to your parties than your other guests do. The next time you host a celebration, write on each guest's name tag a notable fact about her. You might want to check with your guests to be sure that they don't mind having others know that fact. For example, one of your friends wrote a book in four days, was the only man to participate in a muffin bakeoff, holds the record for catching the largest sailfish off the coast of Baja, or invented a bed for paramedics to use to transport victims of mountaineering accidents. Your guests will love learning about other guest's accomplishments and you'll enjoy helping to spread their fame. ☺

291 Create a Theme Party Quiz with a Prize to Get People Sharing Answers

You could talk for hours about baseball. Or, your knowledge of political trivia is unrivalled. Maybe you've been crowned the winner of previous quizzes about Saint Patrick's Day. Or perhaps you aren't into sports or saints but you know more about music trivia than the average musician. Put together a trivia quiz for a theme party. Print copies to give to your guests. Create goody bags with trivia memorabilia to give the winners. A fun quiz could be the perfect element to get your friends and family engaged in a little friendly competition to see who will reign as the biggest know-it-all this year. ☺

292 Wear Black Fishnet and a Bunny Tail for Your Hubby's Birthday Party

There are some parties when the guest list should be kept really short, say, just the two of you. Your husband's birthday could be one of those occasions when you show him a totally different side of your personality. You don't have to look like the Playmate of the Year, but it might be fun for both of you if you could slip into some fishnet stockings and one of those skimpy little outfits with a bunny tail. If you want to get really crazy, you could cook him a gourmet meal, set the table for two, and then get dressed to meet him when he comes home from work. It might be a good idea to have a sitter care for the kids for a few hours while the two of you rediscover how exciting a birthday party can be. ☺

293 Take Digital Pictures of the Party and Send Them to All Your Guests

You know your upcoming party is going to be a huge success because you've planned it for months. Maybe it's a Halloween costume party, a Mother's Day celebration, or a Christmas office party. Whatever the occasion, don't forget to take lots of pictures with your digital camera. Download the pictures from your camera into your computer so that you have instant access. Pick out the top five and e-mail them to all the guests. When people have enjoyed each other's company, they also enjoy reliving the moment viewing photos of everyone having a wonderful time. Do your part to spread the happiness. ☺

294 Ask Three Friends to Serve as Your Postparty Cleanup Crew

Parties are fun, but the cleanup often is not. If you hate doing the cleanup alone, enlist the help of three or more friends to help you do all those cleaning chores. The work goes much faster when more than two hands are doing the work. Your friends will appreciate your trust in them to help you and they know that they can call on you the next time the party is at their houses. And you never know—the postparty cleanup gathering could turn out to be as much fun as the original bash. ☺

CHAPTER 17

Let Happiness Flow from You to Your Community

295 Buy a Homeless Person or Family a Hot Meal

Doing good deeds for others makes you happy, according to happiness experts. It's not easy to know if someone is homeless or hungry. Passing the same family sitting on the park bench during your early morning run each day could suggest their dire circumstances. A distressed veteran asking for help with a cardboard sign on a street corner puts a face on America's often invisible problem of homelessness. Many homeless people have no jobs or money for meals. If their cause speaks to your heart, carry some cards containing a list of local shelters and soup kitchens and pass them out. Buy a hot meal for someone who is hungry. Read about other things you can do at *www .justgive.org*. Find the joy of doing something to ease the suffering of others and give them a dose of happiness, too. ☺

296 Count Your Loose Change and Donate It

For a quick dose of happiness, gather up that loose change lying around the house and give it to a good cause. By some estimates, the average American household has as much as $90 lying under the sofa cushions, in dresser drawers, and even in laundry room where a lot of it comes out in the wash. There are myriad ways to donate your loose change—drop the coins into charity boxes in grocery store checkout lines, give it to your church or temple, or simply convert it to currency and donate it to a favorite charitable organization. Happiness researchers say that when you perform a selfless act of generosity for someone else, it increases your happiness. ☺

297 Make a Green Bean Casserole and Give It to a New Neighbor

Some relative or other always brought a green bean casserole to Thanksgiving dinner or the annual family reunion because that green bean casserole is one of those comfort foods that many American families associate with gatherings of family and friends. A cherry pie, a chocolate cake, a loaf of banana nut bread, mashed potatoes, and, of course, that old standby, the green bean casserole reminds us of a bygone era when life seemed simpler and easier. Back in the day when people didn't have computers, they made friends the old-fashioned way, face-to-face. Why not start a tradition in your neighborhood by giving the green bean casserole to someone who has just moved in. Welcome them warmly and nurture the relationship as it grows. ☺

298 Organize a Daily Walking Group

As you meet neighbors on your daily walks, invite them to join you the next day. Ask them to invite other neighbors or friends to also join your group. Keep the group together by reinforcing the collective effort to live healthy and make good lifestyle choices. Always be on time for your scheduled walk. Share healthy recipes, information about organic foods, and personal goals. Set some goals as a group, such as walking for a mile together and then increasing it to two miles. Or, set a time, say, thirty minutes each day and increase it to forty-five and then sixty. You and your group could even join a charity walkathon to raise money and awareness of the need to find a cure for breast cancer, leukemia, or some other noble cause. ☺

Let Happiness Flow from You to Your Community

299 Play Bridge with Three Friends Once a Week

Happiness experts have established that a strong support network is vital to higher life satisfaction levels. Humans were made for loving others. It is from our relationships with spouses, lovers, and friends that we derive meaning and happiness. Having a group of friends to do things with on a regular basis is a path to happiness. So get the cards, call up three friends, and start having some fun playing Bridge or another card game. ☺

300 Take a Girlfriend Along on Your Monthly Casino Trip

If you enjoy the occasional visit to a casino for a little gambling and a show, double your pleasure and take your girlfriend along on your next trip. Conversation during the trip can break the monotony. Plus, you'll have a pal with you to share your elation at winning or to commiserate with if you lose. Then, of course, there are all those wonderful buffets, and who wants to eat alone? Pleasures of the moment are in abundance when you are enjoying eating a good meal or gambling. Of course, winning at your game also contributes to your levels of pleasure and happiness. You feel happy when you think of all the things you can do when you win a big jackpot. So, if you have a few bucks to spare and some free time, call your gal pal and head off for a pleasurable weekend at the casino. ☺

301 Spearhead a Gourmet Dinner Club

Orchestrate a dinner party for friends who like great-tasting food. If you have a lot of fun at that dinner, suggest that the group form a gourmet dinner club that regularly gets together on a rotating basis in each friend's home. Remind everyone that planning and preparing a gourmet meal or finding appropriate wine is not necessarily as difficult as one might imagine. Every day, the Food Network brings extraordinary chefs into your living room to show you how. Most of those chefs say it starts with fresh, wholesome ingredients and a few basic pantry staples. Wine merchants are happy to help you find the perfect wine accompaniment for your food selection. Sharing food is about more than just eating and drinking; you are sharing meaningful and pleasurable moments of your life with friends who are important to you. ☺

302 Organize a Neighborhood Holiday Progressive

Get into the holiday spirit this year and include neighbors on your street. In December, ask five neighbors to join with you in hosting a progressive dinner party that begins at one house for the first course and proceeds to other houses for subsequent courses. Suggest that your neighbors select one out of five possible courses to host at their homes: appetizers, soup, salad, entrée, or dessert. Then put flyers out at each house on your street inviting all your other neighbors to join in the festivities. Each family who will attend is asked to contribute one item to one of the courses. Be sure to inform everyone to RSVP so that you can keep a running tally of how many people will participate. A number of religious and cultural holidays occur in the month of December so even if the neighbors on your street are from differing ethnic and cultural backgrounds, you can still get them together for a progressive party and some wholesome family fun. ☺

303 Attend Alliance Française or Other Language Social Club

You know what they say about language—use it or lose it. Are you a Francophile? Do you love all things French? Did you study French in high school or college? Doesn't it make perfect sense then to cultivate friendships with others who share your passion for French culture? One way to find some new friends is to attend meetings of social clubs with a focus on French language. There, you can hear guest speakers, learn information that perhaps you didn't know about French history, language, and culture. Oh, and you can practice your language skills if you're not filling your mouth with delicious petits four that someone brought to the meeting. ☺

304 Spend the Afternoon at a Bookstore or Coffee Shop

Book lovers adore bookstores. They also enjoy a cup of good coffee or tea while they read. It's no accident that while many book shops have added refreshment areas where you can purchase a cup of your favorite coffee or tea, coffee houses also sell newspapers and, in some cases, books that the shop is promoting. So, if books are your thing, head off for a delightful afternoon of reading and sipping at a local bookstore. Get to know others who share your passion for literature. It's a good thing to widen your circle of friends. Happiness is doing what you love with others who love doing the things you do. ☺

305 Ask Someone in Your New Class to Study with You

For those times when you want someone to quiz you or share notes from that last lecture, nothing beats a classmate willing to study with you. If there is someone in your class or workshop that you find intriguing or is new to the school or program, ask that person to study with you. Say something to spark a conversation. Imagine how welcoming it feels to be in a new environment and not know anyone and then to have a stranger invite you to study. Most likely, that individual will be as supportive of you as you are of him and, of course, you both want to excel. It's a win-win for both of you. ☺

306 Enlist Neighbors into Making a Farewell Gift

A thoughtful way to send off a longtime neighbor who is moving away is to give her a gift that will always remind her of the years of history you shared. If the person leaving loves gardening, ask your neighbors who have gardens to put seeds of favorite plants into white paper envelopes. Tuck the envelopes into a card to give your neighbor on the day she moves. Or if she loves quilting, ask others on your street to contribute either a piece of fabric or a quilting square. Present the stack of fabric unassembled so that the individual leaving the neighborhood can spend happy hours sewing the pieces together in the way that she wants. The gift of seed will produce plants, a yearly reminder of how much you all loved and appreciated her. A keepsake quilt will remind her of the sense of belonging and togetherness you all have shared. ☺

Let Happiness Flow from You to Your Community

307 Go to an Antique Auction with Friends

Do you love antique furniture, art objects, and rugs? Do descriptive terms like Louis XVI, Victorian, William Morris, and Jacobean style get you excited? If you know of an auction house in your area, plan on seeing the items on one of the viewing days preceding an auction. If the auction house has a website, you may be able to view the items there and possibly even place a bid on an item that sparks your passion. Imagine, for example, finally finding and being able to bid on that that seventeenth-century copper gilt crucifix clock that you always wanted. Check out Sotheby's latest catalogue or go online and look at some antique offerings from different auction companies. Ignite your passion for antiques, invite a friend or two along for the fun, and go in search of that piece of history you hope to find and claim. ☺

308 Join a Political Action Group

Are you dissatisfied with politicians? Do you hope for change? Do you hold a brighter vision for America and the world? Mahatma Gandhi once advised people to be the change that they wanted to see in the world. That means to get off the couch, away from the television, and go out into the world and do something to bring about that change. Join with others who feel as passionate as you about creating a more meaningful life and a better future through political action. Living and working toward a more meaningful and purpose-driven life is an important path to achieving happiness. ☺

309 Use Your Web Pages or Blog to Invite Correspondence

Blogging, short for Web logging, provides a venue for putting your message into the world and to generate responses to your message by readers. Some people refer to blogs as online journals while others consider a blog as a collection of images, messages, data, or media objects that once posted can be viewed via a browser. A blog's postings are usually in chronological order with the most recent entries appearing first. Blogging can be an effective way for you to express your passion and focus on whatever it is that causes you to feel joy. You can even use your blog to generate income. When your interest or passion dovetails into a subject that readers care about, your blog is more likely to draw responses from readers and, thus, grow. So give blogging a try. ☺

310 Attend a Music Camp

What would summer be without music camps? Do you love to play the saxophone? Keyboards? Electric violin or guitar or drums? How about singing for the opera or musicals? Check out music camps offered in your region of the country. They aren't just for kids anymore. Some focus on a single instrument. Others are geared toward chamber orchestra or band music. If you are a beginner, there are camps for adults who are just beginning to think about music for themselves. Some camps are associated with competitions. Many offer scholarships if you can't afford to attend. To find one that is right for you, search for "adult beginner music camp." Nurture your aspiration to learn music because it will be a source of joy throughout your life. ☺

Let Happiness Flow from You to Your Community

CHAPTER 18

Find Happiness
Helping Children

311 Volunteer to Help Sick Kids

If making a positive contribution to the lives of sick children and their families would bring meaning to your life and give you some enjoyment knowing you are helping others, consider donating some time each week to work as a volunteer in a children's hospital or on a hospital's pediatric, neonatal, or nursery wing. People who serve as volunteers in children's hospitals are often a dedicated, committed group from diverse socioeconomic and cultural backgrounds. Hard-working volunteers are always needed and appreciated by hospital staff, the patients, and their families. When you give friendship and compassion to others in their time of need, some say it flows back to you in abundance. ☺

312 Become a Big Brother or Big Sister

If you enjoy the company of young people and could mentor a child, consider contacting Big Brothers, Big Sisters. It is the oldest mentoring organization in the United States, has facilities all over the country, and has been serving young people, ages six through eighteen, for more than a century. National research statistics published by the organization assert a positive enduring impact upon the lives of children who are mentored through that program. For example, many have better family relations, become more confident about doing schoolwork, and are less likely to skip school. In addition, a large percentage of those children and teens involved in Big Brothers Big Sisters are 27 percent less likely to use alcohol and 46 percent less likely to begin using illegal drugs. The time you spend mentoring could optimize a young person's chances for academic success and be a source of happiness for you and everyone involved in that child's life. ☺

Find Happiness Helping Children

313 Become a Soccer Mom

Introducing your children to soccer may end up costing you a lot of time, but you might soon feel it is worth every minute. You can learn a lot about your child and her friends when you are the one transporting them to their soccer matches. But besides having a front row seat to their conversations, you can feel confident knowing that they have a safe driver to shuttle them to and from games. Most likely, your children will appreciate the fact that their mom or dad cares enough to drive them to all those practices. Although at times, it may feel like drudgery, when your children are teenagers and can drive themselves, you'll be able to look back and feel happy knowing that you chose not to miss out on those moments before they could drive. ☺

314 Volunteer to Coach a Youth Swim Team

Not all team sports have to be formally organized through a school, church, or park and recreation department. If you have the backyard pool and all the children in the neighborhood hang out there anyway, give an added dimension to their fun in the pool by organizing them into swim teams. Encourage them to demonstrate a competitive spirit while helping them develop an appreciation for good sportsmanship. Share in their joy as you watch them evolve as individuals and team players. ☺

315 Take Timeouts to Bond Through Play

Children are expert in the art of play, and they are natural born teachers. If you are feeling stressed out, overworked, doggedly tired, take a timeout for play. It strengthens the parent/child bond. Don't remember how? Playing with your baby or toddler can get you laughing, relieve stress, increase spontaneity, and inspire creativity. You probably don't require a child development expert to explain to you what floor time is. Get down on the same level as your youngster and give your full attention to him or her. Permit your child to lead the way for your own inner child to come out. ☺

316 Build a Tree House for Your Child and the Child in You

If you've got a tree in your yard strong enough to support a tree house, get the children in your family involved in helping you create the overall design, shop for the wood and nails, and help you build it. Not only will your children love you for creating something that will surely give

them many pleasurable hours of fun and memories to last throughout their lives, but you'll create a special space to share with them the child in you. ☺

317 Help a Child Develop a Hobby

Young children, especially boys, it seems, love to play with cars, trucks, boats, and airplanes. If you've ever watched a seven- to ten-year-old child operating a remote radio-controlled car (also called an RC car), you probably noticed that sooner or later a group has gathered, much to the child's delight, to watch the fancy vehicle maneuvers that he orchestrates through a hand-held controller. Some middle school and high school science teachers have used RC cars as tools for teaching radio-control robotics and programming. Encourage your children to express their interests and develop them into hobbies. You'll enjoy helping them while they are young, and you'll be even happier if, as young adults, they decide to pursue meaningful careers in academic disciplines such as science. ☺

318 Donate Your Shoes to Benefit a Child

Did you know that you can make a difference in a child's life by just cleaning out your closet? Many children in certain regions of the United States (such as in Appalachia) do not have even one pair of shoes. A decent pair of shoes is important where cuts and scrapes and splinters could become a health risk, especially in places where there is little or no possibility of receiving medical care. Whether a child has been the victim of poverty, natural disaster, domestic violence, or abuse and neglect, receiving a pair of shoes—a basic necessity—can ensure that his feet are protected. Your donation of money and/or your children's shoes or new child-size shoes enables Soles-4Souls to provide footwear to children who are in desperate need. Think about how happy you will feel knowing that the shoes that your children had outgrown and that were gathering dust on a closet floor have found another home. That's something to be truly happy about. Check out *www.soles4souls.org*. ☺

319 Read Funny Books to Kids

If you love to read, spend some time reading to children. You can read books to kids anywhere—at home, at a local library, an infant and∂ toddler daycare center, a nursery school, a doctor or dentist waiting room, in a hospital waiting room, or even at clubs for kids such as Cub Scouts or Brownies. Just be sure that your book is appropriate for the age group. A funny book will inspire laughter and you'll likely laugh, too, because the happy laughter of children is infectious. ☺

320 Sponsor a Child

Make a difference in the life of a child by choosing to sponsor a child. You might choose sponsorship through an established charitable organization like World Vision, Children International, or Save the Children, which provides schooling, medical care, and training in economic opportunities for a disadvantaged child's family. Many children in the world struggle daily to survive. They don't have even the basic necessities. Your commitment and support will literally change a child's life and add meaning and purpose to yours. People who feel their lives have purpose and meaning, according to psychologists and social science researchers, are generally happier and have greater life satisfaction. ☺

321 Foster a Child's Inquisitiveness

Mirror for a child the wonder that life is going on all the time, happening in every moment, and that there are incredible things to notice all the time, all around. Point out the way the light shimmers on dew drops clinging to an elaborate spider's web, the scent of lilacs after a hard rain, the majestic flight of eagles, the taste of a freshly cut watermelon, the pattern of a piece of gum stuck to the pavement, the vibrant color of a peacock feather, or the sizzle of a marshmallow toasted over a crackling fire. Noticing details helps fire a child's imagination and natural inquisitiveness about the world. ☺

322 Cheer a Child Onward to Victory

If you enjoy kids and love seeing them excel in sports and teamwork, show your support. If your school district has youth sports teams that compete with others within your district, go out to the games and be a vocal supporter. Cheer loudly. While the kids appreciate you rooting for them, you can savor the joy of doing something for them that requires a small investment of time and makes you happy. ☺

323 Volunteer to Talk at Your Local High School Career Day

Show your enthusiasm. If you love your job and would like to share your appreciation for your work, contact your local high school and offer to participate in its annual career day. Junior and senior high school students are already thinking about what

their life's work will be, and some are already taking the courses they will need to get on the right track when they enter college to pursue a degree in their chosen fields. You can highlight what you do and what kind of educational background is helpful. Not everyone is fortunate to find work that not only is challenging but meaningful and pleasurable. That's worth sharing. ☺

324 Help a Child Develop Superior Study Habits

Many parents encourage their children to tackle homework right after school when lessons learned during the school day are still fresh. But other parents allow their children to wait until after the evening meal to hit the books. Child educators and development experts say the key to academic success with regard to homework is regularity. Good study habits enforce the sense of self-discipline and responsibility. Try to establish a routine place for doing homework (on the island in the kitchen, desk in the child or teen's room, or dining room table, for example.). Also, establish a particular time when homework is to be done. Don't be a drill sergeant but rather supporting and helpful. Eliminate unnecessary distractions such as televisions, radios, and cell phones (long phone calls or text messaging can eat up hours). Helping your children develop good study habit skills will be an important factor to their future success in school, college, and life. ☺

 Help Families Who Have Children with Autism

If you find happiness helping others, consider reaching out to a family with a child with autism. Such families and their children will need a lot of help in life. About 1 in 150 children has an autism spectrum disorder, according the Autism and Developmental Disabilities Monitoring Network (which includes researchers from a dozen institutions, including the Johns Hopkins Bloomberg School of Public Health). Offer support in whatever ways you can; for example, by driving the parent and child to therapy appointments, shopping for groceries, or babysitting the child so the parents can have a break. ☺

 Introduce Your Child to Other Cultures

Perhaps you enjoy traveling and have already seen and experienced some of the world and have even shared your stories with your child. Take it a step further. On your next family vacation or outing, go someplace where your child can learn about a unique culture. It doesn't have to involve international travel. For example, you could plan a trip to Pennsylvania to see the Amish country, the Four Corners in south-western United States where the ancient Pueblo people lived, or to New York or Connecticut—the ancestral home to the Mohegan tribe of Native Americans. Your child will have amazing stories to share with his friends and classmates and you'll have the happiness that comes from knowing that you've given your little one a gift of a lifetime. ☺

327 Help a Child Develop Respect for Rules and Authority

Children who are taught respect at home are more likely to show respect toward others outside of the home. Explain to them why families and societies need rules, and authority figures to follow and enforce those rules. Help them understand how respect is earned. Demonstrate for them how to show respect through listening atten-tively, valuing others' opinions and ideas, and showing consideration to all. Explain how certain actions like pressuring someone to do something they don't want to do is being disrespectful. Teach your children that when you are respectful toward others, the world is a happier, nicer place for everyone. Let them know that when they are respectful, it makes you happy. ☺

328 Volunteer to Host a Foreign Exchange Student for a School Year

You don't need to leave home to experience another culture. You can open your heart and your home to a student from abroad. When you host a high school, college, or graduate-level student in your home for an academic year, you get more than a just a houseguest. You will be gaining priceless exposure to another culture and family through the exchange program. Welcoming host families that can provide a safe and supportive environment for a foreign student are vital for international exchange programs to work. The happy memories during your host year will likely last forever. ☺

 329 ## Donate a Weekend to Establishing a Teen Neighborhood Center

When you think about your community, do you know whether or not there is a safe place for teens to hang out? If there isn't, think about how you could rally support for one. Creating a teen-designated space starts with one person having the idea and motivation to spearhead the concept. In some communities, teens themselves form a council of representatives from all the schools in an area to raise money, awareness, and a volunteer work force to take the dream to reality. Help teens in your town stay away from gangs, drug and alcohol abuse, and teen pregnancy by creating a place where they can hang out safely and share happy times with friends. ☺

CHAPTER 19

Lead Others to Happiness

 **330** Keep Your Promises to Others

One way to spread happiness is to keep your promises. Just as you see someone who is faithful to her word as trustworthy, so your friends, family, and business colleagues will also trust you when you hold to the truth. In this age of spin, when facts get altered in ways to deliberately mislead people and to further ideological agendas, let your truth be absolute. It isn't always easy to align your feelings, thoughts, beliefs, and spoken words so that no one questions your truthfulness or integrity. Gandhi used truth as his nonviolent weapon against adversaries. No one questioned his truthfulness or whether he could keep his promises to others. Imagine the happiness of millions of Indians when his Quit India movement secured their freedom from the British. ☺

331 Ask Someone to Tell You Her Purpose in Life

If you've ever asked someone what her purpose in life is, you may have gotten a blank stare and silence. It's not like asking people to name their job. They are going through the motions of their lives and they know what they do every day, especially at their places of employment, but the word in your question that throws them off is "purpose." Purpose is the reason for doing something or why it exists. Working at a job is necessary to earn money to support yourself and your family, but it isn't your purpose. Living purposefully means much more than your job. Here's a hint—it likely will have something to do with love, compassion, peace, consciousness, truthfulness, meaning, awakening, and courage. Figure out your purpose and then spark a dialogue on that topic with others. As you already have learned, people are happiest when life for them has meaning and purpose. ☺

Lead Others to Happiness

332 Work at an Orphanage and Demonstrate Happiness to Children

A child orphaned as a result of war, famine, or disease may bear many scars that are not easily healed. But you can help him trust again and feel hope. Perhaps one day he'll smile or laugh and be able to feel happy. You may not know that volunteering to work at an orphanage also can gain you some college credit. Of course, it will depend on the program. For example, the Institute for Field Research Expeditions (IFRE) places volunteers and interns in eighteen countries in Africa, Latin America, and Asia. That organization has in-country staff and facilities to support you and your work abroad. Check it out at *www.ifrevolunteers.org*.

Likewise, Serve Your World needs volunteers to work in orphanages in Guatemala, Africa, and the Philippines. Similarly, in Peru, the Puericultorio Perez Aranibar, the largest children's home in South America, needs people to provide child care for infants and toddlers, teach conversational English to teens, or work with older children on maintenance projects. Your work can help spread a little happiness to the most vulnerable children who have been living on the street, are abandoned, orphaned, or disabled. ☺

333 Accompany Your Child's Class on School Field Trips

Your child or her teacher may have asked you to help as a parent volunteer on an upcoming school-sponsored field trip. Often, schools need parent volunteers to accompany the children to field trip destinations such as a natural history museum or historic or cultural sites. If you can get the time off from work or other commitments, consider volunteering for at least one of the field trips during the school year. It allows you to see firsthand what your child is experiencing during the field trip and how and what she is being taught. It also will mean a lot to your youngster that you have taken time off to join her and her classmates. For some kids, that's a really big deal and a source of happiness and pride. ☺

334 Draw Others to Happiness Through a Church or School Fundraiser

Demonstrate a sense of joyful purpose in helping your church, school, and community meet their fiscal responsibilities through fundraising efforts. There are hundreds of articles about fundraising on the Internet and reading about what's involved is always a good place to start the process. Success in church fundraising depends, in part, on building a bond between the fundraising campaign and

the church's community, showing need, and having a donor recognition program that reinforces a sense of belonging. School fundraising events work best when the "fun" in fundraising is emphasized. Some ideas for school fundraisers include seasonal events, food or juice booths, candy product sales, car washes, and card sales (for prepaid phone cards, pizza, or local shop gift cards). Church fundraising ideas include bake sales, holiday boutiques, bingo, and raffles. Raise some money for your church or school and spread the concept of how helping others can bestow happiness on all involved. ☺

335 Refuse to Engage in Malicious Gossip

Count to ten and tell your friend that you're breaking the gossip habit. Counting is one of those techniques you can use to manage a behavior that you choose to avoid. It's a powerful technique in anger management and can also be used when you don't wish to gossip. Malicious gossip is mean, and some experts declare it nothing less than a form of bullying. Step back, count to ten, and remove yourself from the gossip clique. Don't take part in the mudslinging. Feel happy knowing that you didn't and your friend might see the error of it as well. Finding things to praise about others inspires people to feel happy whereas gossiping does just the opposite. ☺

336 Sign Up to Work at a Shelter for Runaway Teens

Teens run away from home for a variety of reasons, some more compelling than others, but they may not be aware of the dangers they face living on the streets. Experts on crime and teen runaways point out that teens are seldom running to somewhere to have fun. Rather, they are running away from bad home situations and family problems that might be precipitated by divorce, job loss, sexual abuse, drug and alcohol abuse, and physical abuse. Crisis hotlines and teen shelters are necessary for assisting these young people who are not yet adults and who have no means of support. If this cause resonates with you, check out *www.standupforkids.org* or volunteer at a local teen shelter. Generate happiness, as much as possible, in that young person's life. ☺

337 Give a Book to a Friend to Motivate or Inspire Him

If you know someone who can't seem to get going, is a little down, or has lost interest in things that used to excite him, give him a book that you have found inspiring or motivational. Talk with that individual about the reasons that life is no longer happy and fulfilling for him. See if you can find out what precipitated the loss of interest. Perhaps that person needs more than a book; it might be necessary to suggest that he seek professional counseling if he's depressed. Ask yourself what you might do to help him get interested in life again. Would a motivational support group help him? Would he like to attend church, temple, or a meditation group with you? Is he burned out from work and does he need a weekend or longer away? If so, invite him to join you for some rest and relaxation, a vision quest, or a spa getaway. Just as you might during dark times in your life welcome a shoulder to cry on, a helping hand to lift you, or someone to walk with you when you feel alone, your friend may need that from you now. ☺

338 Suggest Three Goals to Help a Family Member Strive to Be the Best

Perhaps your ten-year-old son struggles to keep up with his peers in math, your younger sister has body-image issues, or your spouse recently was denied that promotion he was promised. Let them grapple with their issues but be their cheerleader. Remind them that there are good alternatives to blaming or feeling self-pity. Point out what is truly unique and special in them. During times when loved ones are down, you can cheer them on to success. In a frank and loving discussion, help them figure out three goals that will enable them to be better at what they aspire to do and to also have a healthier self-image. ☺

339 Spend an Hour Listening to Someone Discuss Life's Struggles

If you know an individual who is going through difficult times or who lives alone without much social contact, donate an hour of your free time to listen to her talk about life and the difficulties she faces. Humans need social contact, but not everyone's life circumstances allows for such interaction. Your company, even for an hour, can raise someone's spirits. Your time of listening can mean a lot to someone who believes there is no one in the world who cares if she lives or dies. You don't have to solve her problems, but just be a supportive and sympathetic listener. Your company might enable her to relieve some of the pressure she feels in her ongoing life struggles. You take brightness into her life through the generosity of your time and thoughtfulness. ☺

340 Inspire a Negative Person to Think Positively

If you have a family member or friend who is always negative, try to understand why he interprets everything in the worst possible light. Show him a more positive way of viewing the world. For example, maybe your husband is complaining that his daughter wrote on his Father's Day card that she loved him, but also asked why was he always so negative. Empathize with his hurt feelings first, and then try to discuss (without judging) how his personal views are affecting his relationships with her (and maybe everyone else). Work out a plan that you can implement together to help him develop a more positive take on things. ☺

341 Tell a Story to Inspire Someone Who Is Feeling Down

Your personal stories can inspire someone to achieve success or to believe in herself, overcome adversity, or just feel a little happier when her mood is dark. Comforting someone lost, alone, or sad is a way of expressing your spiritual or religious belief and spreading happiness. You can help an individual displace the negative energy in her life with something positive. A personal story can help people who have lost hope to regain control of their lives and begin to search for answers to their own problems or find new meaning. Let your stories help others appreciate their own positive qualities rather than their accomplishments. ☺

342 Attend an AA Meeting if You Have Recovered and Can Share Insights

Recovering from an addiction is an ongoing process that requires a lot of work. But even before the work begins, the addict has to have the courage to admit he has a problem. Alcoholism is a disease that requires treatment by professionals, people who understand the many facets of addiction and who can help break the addiction cycle. If you have recovered, attend an AA meeting and offer to tell your personal story and insights about beating the addiction. Be a friend or a sponsor for someone who is trying to reclaim his life. Your story can lift and inspire another to stay on the path to health, wholeness, and happiness. In you they see an exemplar for making good choices. ☺

Lead Others to Happiness

343 Interview Happy People for an Article That Shares Their Tips

When you meet people who are positive-thinking and content with their lives, ask them what makes them feel that way. Ask them if you can interview them as part of the research effort you are doing for an article about happy people. Pose questions in a way that will draw out their answers—not simply as yes or no—but rather as long and thoughtful responses. Encourage them to share their tips for cultivating a happy life. Then, work up a short article about what you've learned and see if you can get your local newspaper or neighborhood flyer to print it. ☺

344 Tell a Loved One or Friend That You Are Proud of Her

The statement, "I am proud of you," is something people don't hear very often. Yet hearing it does so much for the hearer's self esteem. It should never be a substitute in families for the words, "I love you," but rather reinforce your bonds with children, lovers, and friends. Be generous with your encouragement and praise. It costs you nothing and can mean happiness for those who hear it. Show through your example that happiness isn't success, lots of money, the latest model of car in your garage, or having your child graduate from MIT. ☺

CHAPTER 20

Discover Ways to Spread Happiness in the World

345 Spread the Word about Eco-Shopping

If shopping makes you happy, just think how good you'll feel shopping for goods that are eco-positive; meaning that they have been created in ways that have a positive impact on people and the planet and do not harm animals. And telling your friends, business associates, and relatives to do the same means you will be spreading happiness around your community and elsewhere. For thousands of products, go to *http://world ofgood.ebay.com*. ☺

346 Think of Three Things You Can Do to Make the World a Better Place

Think of three things you can do that don't cost money but

that can benefit the world. You could pick up trash along your daily walk. With the rainforest disappearing at an alarming rate, you could plant a tree or two. Recycle, if you don't already. Hold open a door for a mother with a small child and a stroller. Give a laborer a fresh bottle of water when he's working up a sweat. Implement as many ideas as you can and feel the joy of knowing that you are truly making the world a better place, one selfless action at a time. ☺

347 Speak Thoughtful and Caring Words or Don't Speak at All

With a little effort, you can retrain your impulse to blurt out commonly used negative words and phrases in your speech in favor of using positive words that are carefully chosen and thoughtfully offered. For example, phrases like, "there's always room for improvement," "I've seen better from you," or "good enough, but no cigar" are not helpful and, in fact, suggest that someone's actions or thoughts have come up short and don't meet your expectations. You don't want to hear that kind of response, so stop when the impulse arises to say it. Consider positive, helpful feedback and comments. Speak honestly but caringly so as to inspire greatness from others and generate happiness during the process. ☺

348 Join the Fight to End All Child Labor

If you are outraged by child labor in places like China, India, Uganda, or Togo, join forces with humanitarian and legal organizations, grassroots groups, and concerned coalitions to end such illegal and inhumane practices. A crime in many parts of the world, child labor nevertheless continues. In the handmade carpet industry of Asia, children, whose small hands are best suited for making tiny knots, are often trafficked or kidnapped and sold into debt bondage to work in factories. They made be paid half an adult worker's wages yet work for long hours and without proper food or drink. Hazards to their health are many, including respiratory problems (from inhaling fibers), skin punctures from working with sharp tools, and even deformities and impaired vision. The carpet industry is only one of many that use child labor. If this cause speaks to your heart, get involved in making a difference in a child's life. Lend your voice and support to those pressuring all countries of the world to abolish child labor. ☺

349 Join an Organization That Works to Secure World Peace

In light of the armed military conflicts being waged in hot spots throughout the world, peace seems like a complicated issue. Yet, some would say that peace begins with you, the individual. Exemplars of peace include the spiritual leaders like Buddha and Jesus and social reformers and pacifists like Mohandas K. Gandhi and Martin Luther King Jr., among others. All were visionaries who rallied others around them through their ideas of love, compassion, and harmony. Achieving peace, it seems, will take individuals in great numbers to stand up for and demand peace as a fundamental human right. The Dalai Lama said that peace has to begin first with each person finding inner peace. Join those who believe that, as citizens of the global community, peace is pre-eminently important. Work for a culture of peace and happiness, not just for the few but for everyone, everywhere. ☺

350 Ask Five Colleagues to Help You Sponsor a Single Mom's Education

Your efforts to get others to help you sponsor a single mother's college education could make a huge difference in her quality of life and in the lives of the children she is raising alone. For a single mom, getting a degree or professional certificate may seem impossible, a fantasy. Many single mothers work multiple jobs just to feed and clothe their brood. Often they live paycheck to paycheck and hope they don't get sick. Yet they frequently catch the colds and illnesses that go around because their fatigue and stress reduces the ability of their immune systems to fight off such opportunistic infections. Many do not have health insurance. Research supports the idea that higher education for single mothers benefits society. You don't have to do it alone; ask five business colleagues or friends to join your effort. ☺

 351 List Three Things You Can Do to Help a Homeless Veteran

You see them, sometimes in wheelchairs with limbs missing, sleeping in shelters, under bridges, in alleyways, or abandoned buildings— places where they can escape inclement weather and where they can feel safe enough to close their eyes. There are roughly 46,000 homeless veterans today who have been classified as chronically homeless, according to the National Coalition for Homeless Veterans. The U. S. Department of Veterans Affairs claims that four percent of them are female. For more information, see *www.nchv.org*. Helping veterans to find affordable housing, access to health care, and earn a livable income are three things you and your members of your community could do to help. Think of three other things in your power to improve the life of someone who has served this country and then do them. ☺

 352 Sing, Teach a Class, or Give a Talk at a Senior Citizen Center

You may know of someone, perhaps even a family member, living in a retirement community, an assisted-living facility, or a nursing home. Many such facilities have a center where residents may gather for special programs or for planned social events and activities. You can spread some good cheer by volunteering some of your free time to a senior center to give a talk, organize a music recital, lead a songfest, lecture, or teach a class. Today's senior citizens are not quite like previous generations of seniors. They like stimulation, care about good health, eat right, appreciate lifelong learning, and enjoy socializing, even if their options are limited to conversations with others living in their community. Most likely, whatever you do will be appreciated and the topic of happy conversation long after you've done your bit. ☺

353 Create a Happiness Blog on Your Website

Consider adding a blog on your website in which you journal every day on the subject of happiness. Blogging is a way of creating a lens for yourself and those who read and respond to your ideas about happiness. A daily focusing on happiness, which ebbs and flows according to your thoughts, moods, actions, health and well-being, will teach you more about happiness than just reading a book or trying on other people's ideas. ☺

354 Make Holiday Cards Using Happiness as Your Theme

You can use happiness as your theme for any special occasion for which a card is appropriate, but the happiness focus works especially well for holiday cards. Create a handmade card for birthdays, anniversaries, engagements, christenings, and other occasions, too. Craft stores carry blank cards and envelopes. You can use calligraphy and water color or tempera paint to create appropriate images, or design your card on your computer and print it on card stock. Implicit in your unique card are messages of caring, thoughtfulness, and, of course, your wishes for abundant happiness. ☺

355 Design a "Be Happy" T-Shirt to Sell on eBay

Iron-on transfers are easy to produce and apply on T-shirts that you can then sell over the Internet. Simply select digital photos or other images and take them to your local copy center to have heat transfers made. If you want to promote your happiness website, blog, charitable cause, or you want to spread a little good cheer with a happiness quote or joke, put it on a T-shirt, get it exposed, and spread the good cheer. ☺

356 Write a Book of Sayings about Happiness by Great Thinkers

If you like research, go online or to the library and find what some of history's great thinkers had to say about the pursuit of happiness. Keep a list, and when you have a few pages, enter them into a computer file. Or, you could find some pretty paper and write each quote using calligraphy. Turn your collection of sayings into a small booklet that you can bind in various ways. For example, you could use a three-hole punch and weave a brightly colored silk ribbon through the holes and use something inspirational for the cover. Your book of sayings can serve as a source of inspiration for those times when you or someone you love slips into negative thinking and can't find happiness and peace of mind. ☺

357 Write a Standup Comedy Routine to Perform

Watch Comedy Central or Saturday Night Live and try writing a little monologue about happiness to perform for your children and spouse. If you have a comedic sense and love to laugh, you might enjoy refining your skit and offer to show it to friends, who, of course, would be willing to critique it. When you get really good, consider taking it into your community, performing it at fundraisers, school and church programs, charitable events, and even a local comedy club. Be fully engaged in the process. The French novelist Colette noted that she had enjoyed a wonderful life and only wished that she had realized it sooner. Enjoy and claim your life's happiness now. ☺

358 Teach a Class on the Art of Laughter Yoga

Learn about laughter yoga, how to do it, and why it can bring you numerous health benefits such as lowering your blood pressure and decreasing the amounts of cortisol and other stress hormones circulating in your blood. That's good for your heart health. When you laugh, you breathe deeper, increasing oxygenation of your cells. Fake laughter, according to laughter yoga teachers, has the same mental and physical health benefits as real laughter. Some studies show that laughter can bring about the release of endorphins (the body's natural hormones that decrease pain), provides a massage of sorts to the internal organs such as the liver and spleen, and often increases the likelihood of having a good night sleep. The average adult may laugh roughly fifteen times each day, but laughing comes naturally to children who laugh up to three hundred times a day. Check out *www .laughteryoga.org*. ☺

359 Volunteer Cook at a Children's Summer Camp

Put your cooking skills to good use preparing food for children at a summer camp. Children need good nutrition to keep them active, healthy, and happy. Unlike a meal thrown together when you are angry or upset, the food you prepare when you feel a sense of well-being, happiness, and love is infused with good vibrations according to yoga practitioners. So cook up something kids will love and serve it to them with a smile. You already know that kids laugh a lot, so a smile or a snicker could be enough to spread the cheer all the way down the serving line. ☺

360 Fight for International Justice

If you feel passionate about human rights and would welcome the opportunity to serve in that field in some way, organizations like Human Rights Watch and Amnesty International may have a position for you. Amnesty International works to raise global awareness of human rights violations, such as in Mexico where one in four women are subjugated to abuse from her partner. The organization is also concerned that rich nations are breaking international aid promises. In addition, Amnesty International seeks a moratorium on the death penalty because people in many countries have not received fair trials, may be innocent, and are facing certain death. If the work of that organization appeals to you, check out *www.amnesty.org*. Bring light back into the life of someone who may be facing darkness alone. Restore his or her joy through your work. ☺

Discover Ways to Spread Happiness in the World

361 Spread Happiness Through E-mail

When you find a happiness quote that you love, put it at the bottom of your e-mail so it will be read by everyone you correspond with throughout your day. Also, when you happen upon funny pictures, hilarious stories, jokes, quips, and quotes that brighten your day, spread the good feelings to everyone in your e-mail address book. If your e-mail recipients are having a bad day, your dose of optimism, humor, and happiness may be just what they need to start giggling and get back into their joyful groove. ☺

362 Spearhead a Community Happiness Forum

Create a community happiness forum to raise funds for your favorite charity or for some other cause that you believe is worthwhile and that gives your life meaning. Bring in the best speakers you can find to talk about the physical and mental health benefits of laughter. Ask clergy members to address the spiritual aspects of happiness. Bring in a comedian, a laughter yoga expert, and psychologist, for example, to create a lens for people to understand the nature of happiness, what it is and isn't, how to achieve happiness, and why it's important for good health and longevity. You might also invite a group of children who are willing to answer the questions, "What makes you giggle? What makes you happy?" Why? Because children laugh so often and their laughter is contagious. ☺

363 Honor a Bride and Groom with a Happiness Toast

Remember the Buddha said that happiness is achieved when your words and your work benefit others as well as yourself. Research the Internet or quote books until you find a humorous quote to use in creating an imaginative and highly personalized toast for newlyweds. You might begin by telling the bride she looks stunning and the groom looks stunned, or something along those lines. Whether you've been asked to offer a toast, provide material for a groom's roast, or write a small wedding speech, make sure that the main thread running throughout is a message containing your best wishes for their lifetime of happiness. ☺

364 Put Happiness Quotes in Fortune Cookies

When you are thinking of innovative ways to spread happiness throughout your world, consider serving a helping of happiness on a plate accompanied by a cup of hot tea. Host a dinner party for family, relatives, friends, business associates, or members of your community or social club. Serve Chinese food. Before passing out the fortune cookies, make sure that you have inserted into each little slips of paper that contain a compliment or a happiness quote. You want to make everyone feel uplifted, happy, and full of good cheer, and you can accomplish that by filling their tummies with great food and their mind with pearls of joy. ☺

Discover Ways to Spread Happiness in the World

365 Spearhead an Eco-Positive Community Action Group

If you see the broken pieces of your neighbor's concrete aggregate driveway being tossed into contractor's bags destined for landfill instead of being run through a crushing machine to make gravel for new construction projects, then get busy organizing a community group that can work together to spread good ideas about ecology in ways that have a positive impact. You and your group could pose questions and offer solutions at meetings of your city council, for example, or start an e-newsletter, or even enlist local environmental groups to help you raise awareness for the need of ecological reform that positively impacts humans and their communities. ☺

APPENDIX

Websites

www.justgive.org:
JustGive.org is a charitable organization that makes charitable giving easy by helping individuals connect to various charities.

www.tolerance.org:
Tolerance.org, a project of the Southern Poverty Law Center, promotes reducing prejudice and teaches tolerance.

www.amnesty.org:
Amnesty International is a global organization of people who campaign for human rights for all.

www.surgeongeneral.gov:
The Office of the Surgeon General oversees the operations of the U.S. Public Health Service and reports to the Surgeon General, America's chief health educator.

www.drweil.com:
Dr. Andrew Weil, M.D., is a leading expert in the field of integrative medicine.

www.hobby.org:
Craft and Hobby Association of America, comprised of professionals working in the craft and hobby industries, works to raise the image of the organization and its members, create consumer demand, stimulate sales, help members succeed, and lead the two industries into the future.

www.un.org:
United Nations is an international group of nations with multiple subsidiary organizations that work toward facilitating common goals such as safeguarding peace, human rights, international security, and open channels of dialogue.

www.adoptapet.com:
Adoptapet.com, a nonprofit organization of pet lovers, works with over 6,000 animal rescue groups of animal shelters to rescue and adopt pets.

www.dogfriendly.com:
Dogfriendly.com is a website that publishes travel guides for dogs, including RV parks, hotels, bed and breakfast lodging, and other dog-friendly places.

www.pet-friendly-hotels.net:
Pet Friendly Hotels is a network of hotels and motels accommodating travelers and their pets.

www.history.uk.com:
History.UK.com is a website dedicated to preserving the background and recipes of historic food and drink in the United Kingdom.

www.soles4souls.org:
Soles4soul.org is a charitable organization that provides shoes to underprivileged children.

Discover Ways to Spread Happiness in the World

www.ifrevolunteers.org:
Institute for Field Research Expeditions is a nonprofit organization that supports authentic research on ecology, poverty, education, disease, and other areas impacting the global community.

www.standupforkids.org:
Stand Up For Kids is a volunteer organization that provides support and aid to homeless and street children by sending volunteers into cities across America to find and help them.

www.nchv.org:
National Coalition for Homeless Veterans is a nonprofit organization that helps community-based service groups provide resources and assistance to homeless veterans.

http://worldofgood.ebay.com:
World of Good.com is an online marketplace for thousands of goods that are eco-friendly and ethnically sourced, including items that are organic or produced in the spirit of fair trade.

www.laughteryoga.org:
Laughter Yoga International is an international movement that uses laughter to achieve health, joy, and world peace.